I0752610

IMAGES
of America

SACRAMENTO'S CHINATOWN

On the Cover: On weekdays, Chinese children attended public school during the day and Chung Wah Chinese School in the evening. The Chinese school ran from 5:00 p.m. to 7:00 p.m. Saturday classes were from 9:00 a.m. to noon. This is the classroom at 522 M Street in the early 1940s. (Courtesy Sally Chan Kan.)

IMAGES
of America

SACRAMENTO'S CHINATOWN

Lawrence Tom, Brian Tom, and the
Chinese American Museum of Northern California

ISBN 9781531653378

Published by Arcadia Publishing
Charleston, South Carolina

Library of Congress Control Number: 2009943769

For all general information contact Arcadia Publishing at:
Telephone 843-853-2070
Fax 843-853-0044
E-mail sales@arcadiapublishing.com
For customer service and orders:
Toll-Free 1-888-313-2665

Visit us on the Internet at www.arcadiapublishing.com

This book is dedicated to the Chinese of Sacramento who for over 150 years have turned adversities into opportunities and in the process succeeded in building better lives for their families and future generations in Gold Mountain.

Contents

ACKNOWLEDGMENTS

The authors owe a great debt of gratitude to the descendants of the pioneer Chinese families of Sacramento who helped make this book possible. We have collected many more photographs than we needed due to the generosity of the people wanting to preserve a part of the history of the Chinese in Sacramento. However, due to the publisher's limitations, we could only use the ones that best focused on the story that we were trying to convey.

In the process, we have made new friends and reacquainted ourselves with old ones. Recognition should be given to the following for their contributions and assistance: David and Jean Chan; Bertha Waugh Chan; Daniel Chan Jr.; Janet Wong Chan, D.D.S.; May Chan; William Henry Chan, M.D.; Thomas Chinn; Jean Chong; Lana Chong; Betty Chan Fong; Eva Chow Fong, Ed.D.; Florence Chan Fong; Jeanette Leong Fong; Joe S. Fong; Joe Wayne Fong; Rob K. Fong; Robert W. H. Fong; Roger G. F. Fong; Wanda Fong; Wil Fong; Holly Fong; Malcolm Gee; Ada Gee; Cynthia Hom Goodman, M.D.; Samuel Ha; Virginia Lim Hashisaka; Dolly Hom; Leonard Hom, Ph.D.; Gena Hoyer; Bill Jang; Easter Jang; Ruth Jang; Calvin Jung; Pastor Ernest Kan; Sally Chan Kan; Robin King; Clara Chan Lai; Jean Fat Lai; Ronald Lai; Hon Lam; Harry Joe Lee; Ruby Lee; Barry Lim; Wei Liu, *World Journal*; Jim and Ruth Lowe; Betty Lee Mar; Sylvia Sun Minnick; Helen Owyang; Hing Owyang Jr., D.D.S.; Julie Thomas of the California State Uuniversity, Sacramento (CSUS) Library Special Collections; Art B. and Barbara Tom; Deborah Jane Tom, M.D.; Kelly Tom; Raymond Tom, M.D.; Irene Kwok Tom, Ed.D.; Wilbur Tom; Frank L. Wong; May Wong; Merrily Fong Wong; Sun Wong; Jimmie Yee; Steve Yee; Doug Yee, D.D.S.; Herbert Yee, D.D.S.; Randy Yee, D.D.S.; Kari Yee; and Mamie Yee.

We also want to especially thank Mary Tom, author Lawrence Tom's wife, for her support and assistance. As a native of Sacramento, she knew many of the people we interviewed, which helped facilitate the whole process. Many times at our initial contact with the contributors, they would greet her first and talk about the past before we started to focus on collecting information for this book.

Unless otherwise noted, the images in this book are courtesy of the Chinese American Museum of Northern California.

INTRODUCTION

Sacramento developed into a thriving river port during the Gold Rush as the entry point to California's northern gold mines. Located upriver from San Francisco (Daifow or Big City), Sacramento's Chinatown or Yee Fow (Second Port or City) was one of the first Chinatowns built in early California. The strategic location of Yee Fow enabled the community to grow quickly into a trade and commercial center for the early Chinese pioneers. Sacramento buttressed its position as an important supply and labor center when it was named as the western terminus of the transcontinental railroad. Many of the Chinese who helped build the railroad settled there, which resulted in a large expansion of the original Chinatown.

Sacramento's Chinatown was established near the Sacramento River along I Street. Restaurants, general stores, laundries, hotels, and opera houses found a home in Yee Fow. Later, as the railroad replaced river steamers, the meaning of the name Yee Fow changed from second port to that of being the second most important Chinatown in California after San Francisco.

BACKGROUND: In order to understand these pictures of Sacramento's Chinatown, it is first necessary to understand Chinese history and Chinese American history. When the Chinese first immigrated to America, China was ruled by foreigners: the Manchus. The Manchus invaded China from beyond the Great Wall and established the Qing (Ching) Dynasty in 1644. After two centuries in power, the Qing Dynasty was under siege, first by the Western powers eager to grab China's riches, and secondly by the Chinese themselves, resentful of being dominated by outsiders. In 1842, England defeated China in the First Opium War. This was the first important sign that the Qing Dynasty would lose the Mandate of Heaven. Soon thereafter, rebellions broke out throughout the country.

Guangdong province, home to almost all the early Chinese pioneers to America, was and still is one of the most prosperous and important provinces in China. Guangzhou, the provincial capital of Guangdong, was the only port open to trade with the West. With this monopoly in trade, Guangdong soon began the development of a rudimentary market economy, creating the infrastructure for international trade, an infrastructure that is still achieving remarkable success today.

Under the guise of the universal right to free trade, England bombarded Guangzhou and started the First Opium War. England's true intention was to secure the right to sell opium to the Chinese, thus enriching their merchants and in turn, their nation. The Qing emperor proved unable to defend China against Western military technology and tactics. After suffering heavy losses, he surrendered.

The defeat of the Qing Dynasty made the Chinese—particularly the Cantonese—recognize that a new world order was in the making. For China to survive, change was essential. The call for change would center on the Guangdong province. Not only had its capital been the first place the Westerners attacked, but Guangdong had the reputation of being the most progressive and rebellious province in the empire. For over 200 years, almost from the moment China was defeated by the Manchus, the Cantonese had formed and maintained a number of "secret societies" (tongs). Each member of a tong made a solemn oath to "Fan Qing, Fu Ming" (Overthrow the Qing, Restore the Ming).

As the Chinese struggled to replace the imperial form of government and respond to the technologically superior Western nations, they received some electrifying news from abroad. Gold had been discovered on the West Coast of America, in a land called California. Many Cantonese saw a chance to strike it rich. Others felt the urge to travel to a new land in search of adventure, much like their ancestors had throughout the Nanhai or South China Sea. Still others saw the possibility of establishing secret societies abroad, free from Manchu spies. Within months, the Cantonese set sail for the Gold Mountain, a land of dreams and unlimited possibilities.

Chinese American History—Myths: The voluntary migration of a people from a non-Western nation to a Western nation was unprecedented in modern world history until the Chinese arrived in California in the middle of the 19th century. This migration took place during the Age of Imperialism when European nations were at the height of their power conquering and colonizing much of the non-Western world. No two civilizations—China and the West—located at the opposite ends of the earth, could be more different from each other. Difficulties were inevitable. From religion to food, clothing, etiquette, government, cultural values, and all other forms of human activity, each civilization had developed along different tracks with little influence from the other. No one knew what would happen, except for one certainty. There would be a monumental clash of civilizations.

This clash would take place in the United States, a rapidly industrializing country based on a democratic form of government, where all people possessed equal rights and were protected by the rule of law. Thus the clash of civilizations between East and West was fought not on battlefields between opposing armies but with laws and within American courtrooms. The challenge for the anti-Chinese or racist side was how to legally discriminate against a minority group in a democracy that abided by the rule of law.

Almost from the time the Chinese first set foot on American soil, they were met by laws that discriminated against them. The Foreign Miners Tax was the first of a long list of laws to discourage the Chinese from coming to America. Shortly thereafter, in 1854, the California Supreme Court held in *People v. Hall* that the Chinese could not testify, thus denying them the right to defend themselves in court. Then state and local governments passed a series of laws restricting the right of the Chinese to earn a living. Legal discrimination against the Chinese reached its high point with the passage of the 1882 Chinese Exclusion Act, which effectively barred all Chinese from immigrating to the United States. In order to gain the votes necessary to pass these laws, the anti-Chinese forces had to create certain myths that later passed as history.

The anti-Chinese version of history is quite simple. Impoverished peasants from the poorest part of China, a land devastated by floods, famine, and fighting, came to America seeking gold in the Gold Mountain. The Chinese were so desperate they were willing to work the worn-out mining claims of others. When the gold gave out, they worked in laundries, as domestic servants, on railroads and farms, taking whatever jobs others did not want. They lived in crowded ghettoes under unsanitary conditions, spending most of the time gambling or using opium. They refused to assimilate because they were sojourners, only coming to America to make some money and return to China.

Anti-Chinese forces created this mythical history while arguing for anti-Chinese laws in legislative hearings convened to determine the merits of enacting these laws. Focusing on the economic conditions in China, these racists justified discrimination against the Chinese on the ground that, no matter how badly the Chinese were treated here in America, they were better off here than there. Arguments that the Chinese would never assimilate supported their position that the Chinese should be excluded and expelled from the United States. The claim that Chinese were "cheap labor" made it appear that the Chinese deliberately impoverished themselves in order to undermine European American labor. This history advanced by the anti-Chinese forces was made to support their position that "the Chinese must go." But history based on distortions cannot long sustain itself.

Forgotten Chinese American History: The gold the Chinese found in California was immense. It helped finance a reform movement and a revolution in China. It revitalized villages in the Pearl River Delta and funded the building of homes, schools, parks, and even a railroad in the emigrant districts. Rather than being driven out of the mines, the Chinese miners were very successful. In 1860, a decade after the start of the Gold Rush, 25 percent of the miners in California were Chinese; by 1870, 58 percent were. When a series of gold rushes took place in other states in the west, Chinese miners, building on their success in California, were among the first to reach the new mining fields. The percentage of Chinese miners in later gold strikes were similar to the percentage in California—Idaho 58 percent, Montana 21 percent, and Oregon 61 percent.

Chinese miners were successful because they could build immense waterwheels and wing dams to control the flow of water and move huge boulders to access the gold lying on the river bottom. They worked in partnerships of more than 100, unlike European American miners who worked by themselves or in small groups. Lacking enough manpower and skill to fully access the gold, many European American miners quit. Rather than being "driven out" or mining the "worn-out" claims of others, the Chinese miners bought or worked claims that others could not handle. This cycle of reworking gold claims continues today as large corporations mine claims abandoned by the Chinese.

Many historians have repeated the story of how Charles Crocker of the Central Pacific Railroad had to convince his superintendent of construction James Strobridge to hire Chinese workers. Strobridge reportedly said that railroad work was too physically demanding for Chinese workers. Crocker responded, "They built the Great Wall, didn't they?" Forgotten was the fact that the Chinese had already proven themselves to be excellent railroad workers when they worked on the Marysville and San Jose Railroads several years before.

The real reason for Strobridge's reluctance to use Chinese workers had little to do with their physical ability. Rather it was because Strobridge, as he readily admitted, was a racist. He refused a direct order from Crocker to hire Chinese workers and told everyone, "I will not boss Chinese." But when the Central Pacific fell behind schedule, Crocker had no choice but to reissue his order to hire Chinese. Of course the Chinese proved to be good workers. Chinese laborers were almost 20 percent of California's workforce at that time, and California employers knew that whenever they needed to find laborers that could do hard physical jobs, they should hire Chinese workers.

Forgotten in the history of the building of the transcontinental railroad is what happened to Strobridge's racist attitude. When Strobridge got the opportunity to "boss" Chinese workers, he gradually gave up his prejudices. By the time the railroad was finished, he had come to respect and appreciate them and called them the best workers in the world. This change in attitude by people working together is perhaps one of the most important lessons to be learned from the building of the railroad.

The anti-Chinese version of Chinese American history labeled the Chinese "sojourners" who only wanted to make a few dollars, then return to China. Yet in American immigration history, no other group fought harder to make America their home than the Chinese. They quickly set roots by building 30 Chinatowns in the first two decades after they arrived. Later, with the passage of the Chinese Exclusion Act, they fought even harder to stay, creating elaborate "paper sons and daughters" plans to circumvent discriminatory exclusion laws. They fought in the courts to stay and become citizens. How aggravating it must have been to these Chinese American pioneers to be told that they were only sojourners.

Forgotten also were the hopes and dreams the Chinese American pioneers had to save China. Starting with the tong secret societies that swore to "annihilate" the brutal Qing Dynasty, the Chinese founded political organizations to help China overthrow the Qing and enter the modern world. The Chinese Empire Reform Association, the Chee Kung Tong, and the Kuomintang were all active in America. The Chinese Empire Reform Association started the Western Military Academy in Los Angeles and opened branch academies in 21 U.S. cities, including one in Sacramento, to train Chinese American soldiers to go to China to fight the Manchus. Later in 1916, Chinese Americans organized the Overseas Chinese Corps of Volunteers and landed a unit of 500 soldiers in Qingdao prepared to march to Beijing and stop an attempt to restore the monarchy. That same year, Chinese Americans in San Francisco founded the Overseas Chinese Military Fund-raising Bureau to support the same goal. Starting in the 1920s, Chinese Americans organized aviation clubs. These clubs purchased planes and trained pilots in 10 American cities. The movement grew after the Japanese occupied Manchuria. In all, over 200 pilots were trained and went to China to fight the Japanese.

A people with a vision cannot be defeated. Besieged by American federal and state governments that enacted discriminatory laws, harassed by a significant portion of the American population who were racist, Chinese Americans did not surrender. They understood that being the first to cross the long and dangerous divide between two civilizations was not for the faint of heart. Whatever adversity they encountered only made them more determined. When the Chinese Exclusion Act was repealed in 1943, they knew that a major battle had been won. When the Immigration Act of 1965 was enacted treating all nations equally, victory in another major battle had been achieved. In 1940, Chinese Americans were a lonely and insignificant minority of 70,000. Today they are the largest Asian ethnic group in America with a population of 3.6 million.

Sacramento's Chinatown and the Future: Sacramento's Chinatown was an important Chinatown, often leading the effort to assimilate Chinese Americans into the majority society. Yee Fow had a different history than the more famous Chinatown in San Francisco. The latter was the center of the anti-Chinese movement, which deeply influenced the treatment Chinese Americans received there. In San Francisco, Chinese Americans were forced to go to a segregated school system and live in a ghetto with strict boundaries. It was possible for a resident to live a lifetime in San Francisco's Chinatown without going beyond its boundaries.

Sacramento's Chinatown was different. Its boundaries were more open and fluid. Its status as the state capital was also important as many Chinese Americans took advantage of the large number of civil service positions that were available in state government. These positions became an important pathway for entry into the middle class.

Another development that smoothed the way for the Chinese Americans in Sacramento to enter the middle class was the grocery store. Sacramento's Chinese American businessmen learned early that to achieve economic success in America, you had to sell to the general public. There were grocery stores in Sacramento's Chinatown from its very beginning, but starting in the late 1920s, these grocery stores in the old Chinatown moved to other parts of the city to serve the general community. After World War II, many of these grocery stores evolved into supermarkets. By 1960, Chinese American–owned stores were 20 percent of the total number of grocery stores and supermarkets in the city, even though Chinese Americans made up only 1.3 percent of the population in the Sacramento area. The combination of the above factors meant that the Sacramento Chinese American community was often at the forefront of assimilation for all Chinese Americans.

For far too long, the narrative of the history of Chinese Americans has been written from a westward frontier perspective that marginalized the Chinese. This may have been understandable during a time when China itself was marginalized. But with China's reemergence on the world scene, China's narrative has changed and that of the Chinese in America must, of necessity, also change. The true history of Chinese Americans is one where two civilizations met on the West Coast of the North American continent. This clash of civilizations did not prove easy, but from a historical perspective, it benefited both sides. The future relationship between China and America is one that is growing more interdependent. By understanding the history of what happened when East met West on the Gold Mountain, there will be a brighter future for both these two great civilizations.

—Brian Tom

One

THE CHINESE HOMELAND

The early Chinese pioneers to America were almost all Cantonese from Guangdong Province. They came from three adjoining districts near the provincial capital of Guangzhou—Zhongshan (Chungshan), San Yi (Sam Yup), and Si Yi (Sze Yup). Eighty percent of the pioneers came from the Si Yi district which included Taishan (Toishan), Kaiping (Hoiping), Enping (Yanping), and Xinwui (Sunwui) counties. Fifty percent were from Taishan county alone. During the first 100 years of their history here, many Chinese Americans traveled back and forth between China and America. But when the Communist Revolution succeeded in China in 1949, contact between Chinese Americans and their ancestral villages was cut off. For more than two decades, it was illegal for Chinese Americans to visit China or even send money back to their families. After Pres. Richard Nixon's historic trip to China in 1972, it became possible for overseas Chinese to once again visit their homeland. Starting in the late 1970s, many Chinese Americans from Sacramento traveled to their ancestral villages. In the 1970s, the villages in the emigrant districts had not changed much from the way they had been 100 years earlier. The main mode of transportation was on foot or by bicycle, food was purchased in street stalls, and housing was the traditional one-story brick row houses without indoor plumbing. The scene has completely changed today. All the emigrant districts are part of the great economic revival of China. Taicheng, the county seat of Taishan, has a five-star resort with world-class food and services. Cars and motorcycles are commonplace, and downtown there is a modern pedestrian mall. Many of the old homes have been torn down, and in their place are multilevel condominiums with air-conditioning, modern kitchens, and baths. Factories and large office buildings have been built on the surrounding farmland. Where once it took an overnight journey by ferry or an all-day bus ride to reach the emigrant districts, today they are connected by expressways to Guangzhou or by hydrofoil to Hong Kong. The modernization that Chinese Americans first learned about in America and hoped for in their ancestral districts has come true.

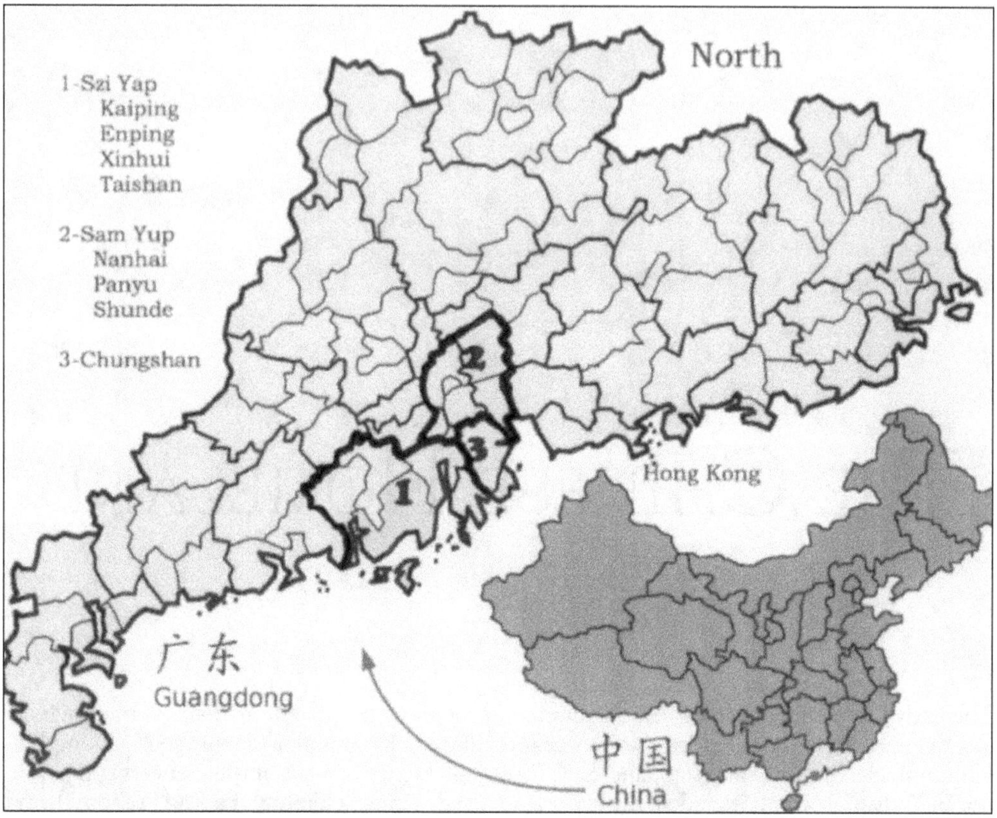

1-Szi Yap
Kaiping
Enping
Xinhui
Taishan

2-Sam Yup
Nanhai
Panyu
Shunde

3-Chungshan

North

Hong Kong

广东
Guangdong

中国
China

Prior to the mid-1900s, most of the immigrants to America were Cantonese from three distinct areas in the Guangdong Province in southern China. This distinction was based on the local dialect spoken in the counties, Sze Yup (four counties), Sam Yup (three counties), and Chungshan (one county). Eighty percent of that immigration came from the Sze Yup counties, and half of those came from just one county, Taishan.

This is the archway into the Xybushan village in the county of Taishan in the Guangdong Province. Archways are typically used as entryways into a village. Xybushan is located directly across the Taicheng River from the center part of the city of Taicheng. Xybushan is a Hom/Tom village. The picture was taken in the early 1990s.

This is the archway to the Taishan Overseas Chinese Museum in the city of Taicheng. This museum tells the story of the overseas emigration from this area. The picture below is a plaque that provides an introduction to that emigration. (Both, courtesy Wilbur Tom.)

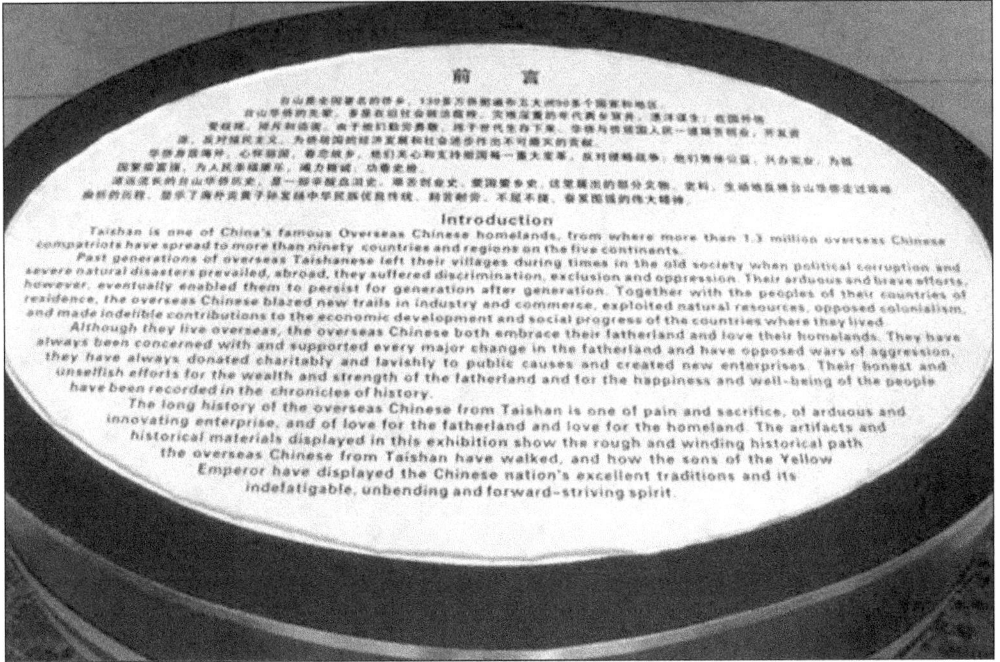

These two exhibits in the Taishan Overseas Chinese Museum display the intense emotions of family members seeing their son and or husband leaving home to search for fortunes overseas. (Both, courtesy Wilbur Tom.)

The use of the Angel Island Immigration Station was started in 1910. All the Chinese immigrants were processed here to determine eligibility for entry into the United States. The picture above shows the administration building and the hospital in the upper center. The picture below shows the detention barracks with the connecting ramp from the administration building. (Both, courtesy National Archives Pacific Region San Francisco.)

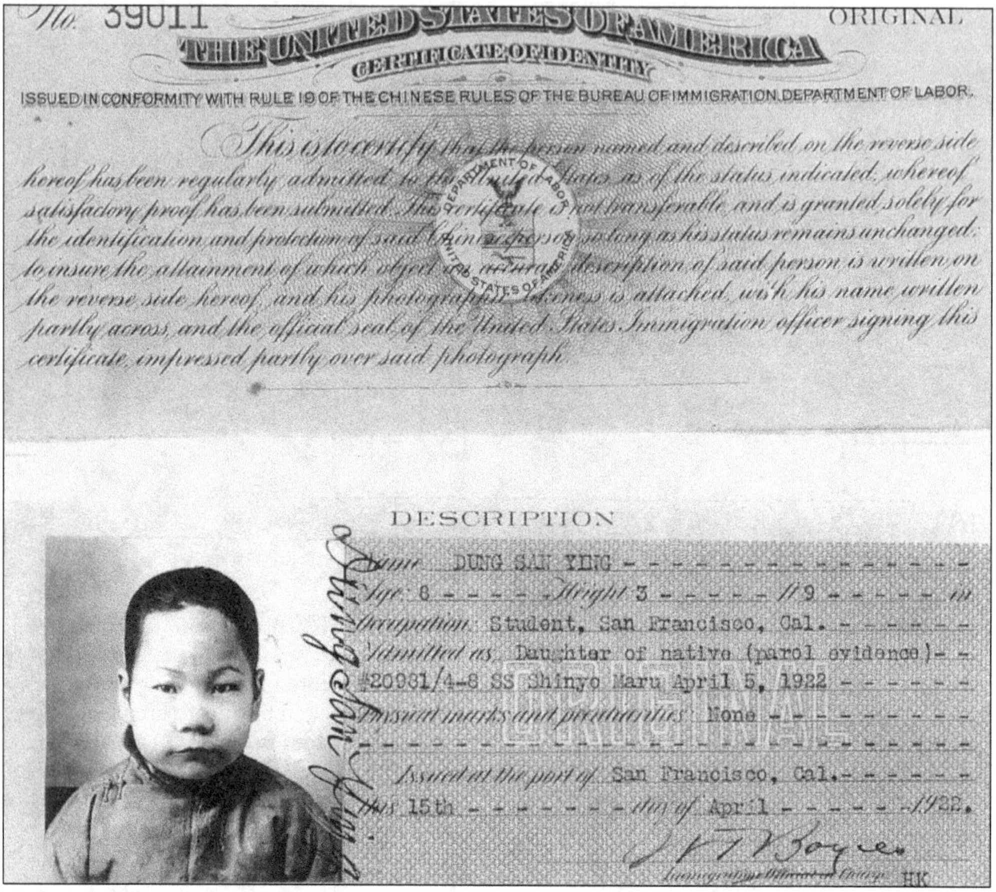

No. 39011 ORIGINAL

THE UNITED STATES OF AMERICA

CERTIFICATE OF IDENTITY

ISSUED IN CONFORMITY WITH RULE 19 OF THE CHINESE RULES OF THE BUREAU OF IMMIGRATION DEPARTMENT OF LABOR.

This is to certify that the person named and described on the reverse side hereof has been regularly admitted to the United States as of the status indicated, whereof satisfactory proof has been submitted. This certificate is not transferable and is granted solely for the identification and protection of said Chinese person so long as his status remains unchanged; to insure the attainment of which object an accurate description of said person is written on the reverse side hereof, and his photographic likeness is attached, with his name written partly across, and the official seal of the United States Immigration officer signing this certificate impressed partly over said photograph.

DESCRIPTION

Name DUNG SAN YING

Age 8 Height 3 ft 9 in

Occupation Student, San Francisco, Cal.

Admitted as Daughter of native (parol evidence) #20981/4-8 SS Shinyo Maru April 5, 1922

Physical marks and peculiarities None

Issued at the port of San Francisco, Cal.

this 15th day of April 1922.

Immigration Officer in Charge HK

This is the Certificate of Identity issued at the entry port of San Francisco for Dung San Ying (Dora Dang), dated April 15, 1922. She immigrated to America in 1922 at the age of eight as the daughter of a native-born American. She married Jang Quin in 1931 and later moved to Sacramento. They had four sons and two daughters. (Courtesy Mary Tom.)

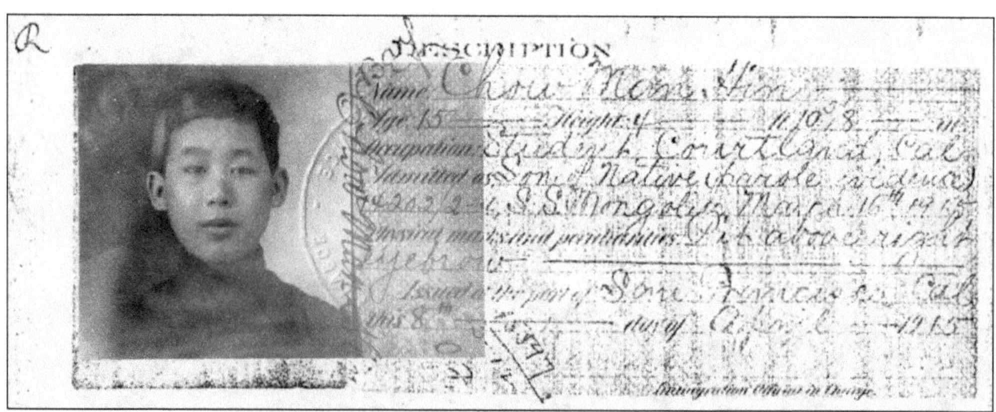

DESCRIPTION

Name Chow Man Hin

Age 15 Height 4 ft 10 5/8 in

Occupation Student, Courtland, Cal.

Admitted as Son of Native (parole evidence)

S.S. Mongolia March 16th 1915

Physical marks and peculiarities Pit above right eyebrow

Issued at the port of San Francisco Cal

this 8th day of April 1915

Immigration Officer in Charge

This is the Certificate of Identity for Chow Man Hin (Chow Chew), dated April 8, 1915. He was born in China in 1899. He immigrated to America at the age of 16 as the son of a native-born American. He worked on a pear farm in Locke. He later became foreman for a labor camp in Lodi. He moved to Sacramento in 1958. (Courtesy Eva Chow Fong, Ed.D.)

Two

Development and Evolution

The Chinese were among the first to arrive in Sacramento after the start of the California Gold Rush. They quickly settled in, building the early Chinatown along the four blocks of I Street between Second and Sixth Streets. It was a male-dominated society filled with newly rich young men looking for a good time. Gambling halls, hotels, restaurants, and houses of ill-repute soon opened to serve these adventure-seekers, making Chinatown a Gold Rush boom town, chaotic and full of life. Sacramento's Chinatown would remain so until the turn of the 20th century, when enough women immigrated to America to start families. Two important developments took place in Sacramento's Chinatown in the 1920s. As more Chinese women came to America, the first true U.S.-born Chinese American generation arrived. The new families created a need for larger homes than those available in Chinatown; thus, many moved to the area south of the original Chinatown. Here Chinese American families lived in an integrated neighborhood and their children attended Lincoln School, an important meeting place. At the same time that Chinese Americans moved away from Chinatown, grocery stores, an important part of Chinatown's business community, expanded outside Chinatown. In another decade, these small grocery stores would develop into small supermarkets. Farmers Market, Bel Air, Giant Foods, and Jumbo Market, all started by Chinese Americans, became household names in Sacramento. These supermarkets acquired a reputation for fresh produce, good prices, and friendly service. The importance of these stores to the Sacramento Chinese American community was that by 1960, twenty percent of the supermarkets and groceries in town were owned by Chinese Americans, though they comprised a much smaller percentage of the total population. The success of the Chinese American grocers and the start of new families led to a change in the residential and vocational patterns of the community. Old Chinatown remained, but its importance as the community center diminished. The trend towards moving to newer neighborhoods with larger houses would continue during the 1940s and 1950s, though the process did not prove easy. Many Chinese Americans encountered racism and had difficulty purchasing homes outside of Chinatown. The discrimination continued until the 1960s, when the old prejudices finally died away.

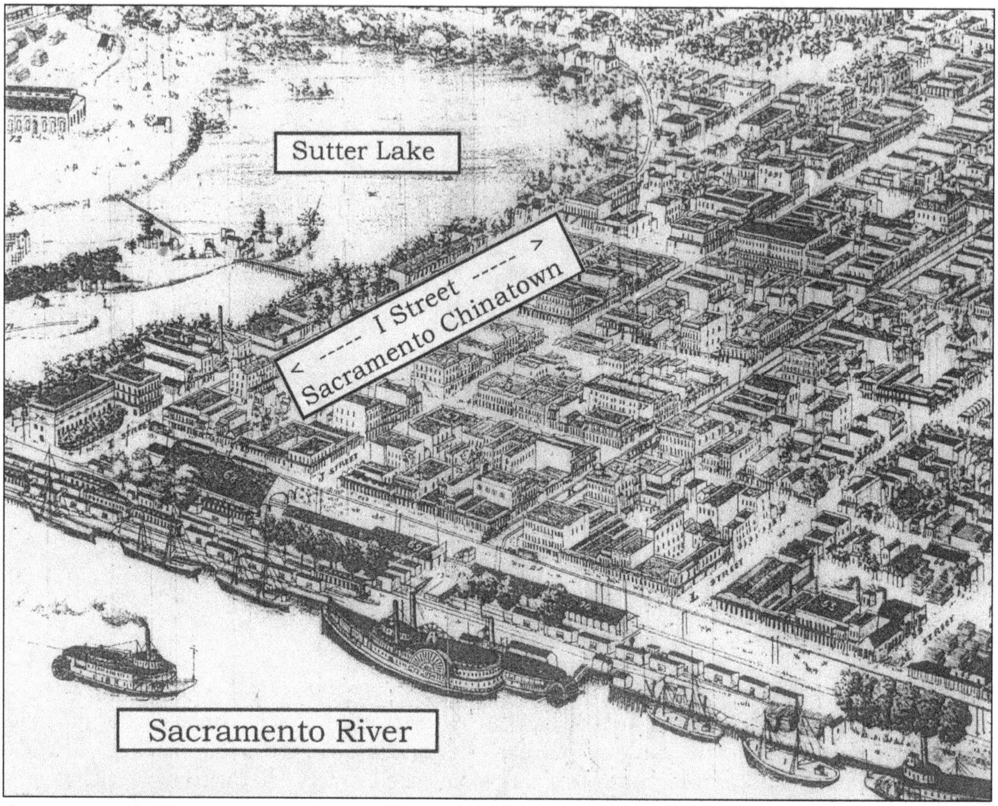

Sutter Lake

< ------ I Street ------ >
Sacramento Chinatown

Sacramento River

Sacramento's Chinatown was initially established on I Street from Second Street to Sixth Street. By the early 1900s, the structures on the north side of I Street abutting Sutter Lake were demolished, and the lake was filled in. The structures on the south side of I Street remained until the start of redevelopment in the late 1950s. This is an 1873 illustration of Chinatown's location. (Courtesy Sylvia Sun Minnick.)

This is the north side of I Street between Second and Third Streets. The barbershop with the striped panels at 215 I Street is owned by Goo Yue Lun. Farther to the right at 221 I Street next to the two-story building was a produce delivery business owned by Chan Kong Sun. This picture was taken in the early 1900s. (Courtesy California Historical Society FN-27730.)

In the 1880 section of the business directory for Sacramento, the Chinese Directory portion listed 97 establishments. There were 44 laundry businesses (referred to here as wash houses). Butcher shops, fish markets, produce stands, and groceries, accounted for 26 of the businesses. The remainders were four cigar store/factories, six tailors, four barbers, two restaurants, six druggists and dry goods stores, and four associations. One was not identified.

CHINESE DIRECTORY
1880

COMPRISING THE NAMES OF CHINESE BUSINESS MEN OF

SACRAMENTO

Ah Coon, cigar store, 306 K
Ah Lee, vegetables, n s I bet 3d and 4th
Ah Lee, wash house, 1131 H.
Ah Lee Som, cigar factory, 902 4th.
Ah Loy & Co., cigar manufactory, 228 I.
Ah Key, wash house, 701 L.
Ah Kung, wash house, Front bet J and K.
CHINESE TEMPLES, cor 2d and I, up stairs, also, N s I bet 5th and 6th and s s I bet 4th and 5th.
CHINESE MASONIC HALL, 501 I.
CHINESE THEATER, e s 3d bet I and J.
CHINESE YOUNG MEN'S CHRISTIAN ASSOCIATION, 905 4th.
Ching Sing, wash house, 1104 4th.
Chung Hing, tailor, 328 I.
Chung Lung, wash house, 1022 J.
Chung Kee, wash house, 1125 2d.
Coon Chang Lung & Co., groceries, 400 I.
Coon Gay, barber, 913 3d.
Eh Heng, barber, 910 3d.
Fong-Lee & Co., groceries and drugs, 229 I.
Fook Hing Low, restaurant, 406 I.
Gee Hop Hing Kee, barber, 223 I.
Goen Kee, fish market, 307 I.
Gin Lee, butcher, 231 I.
Gum Lung, wash house, 1317 2d.
Hand Jim, wash house, 1321 9th.
He Lee, wash house, 224½ I.
Hi Lee, wash house, 1105 3d.
Hop Chung & Co., cigar manufactory, 212 I.
Hip Chung, wash house, 116 K.
Hop Lee, wash house, 1309 K.
Hop Lung & Co., vegetables and fish, 205 I.
Hong Wah, wash house 925 10th.
Hung Lee, wash house, 1023 2d.
Hung Sing, wash house, 31st bet K and L.
Jim Kee, wash house, n s M 8th and 9 th.
John Kee, wash house, 501 O.
Jong Sing, wash house, 1021 10th.
King Hung, wash house, 1427 10th
Kung Sung Chung, groceries, 226 I.
Lane Mow Chung & Co., groceries, 310 I.
Lee Yet, vegetables, 316 I.
Ling Chung, wash house, 1323 3rd.
Loug Sing, wash house, 1005 J.
Long Sing Tai Kee, butchers, 429 I.

Loy Fook Wan, druggist, 227 I.
Lum Kee, barber, 303 I.
Lung Kee, wash house ns J bet 16th and 17th
On Chung, fruits and vegetables, 210 I.
On Kee & Co., grocery store, 404 I.
Own Kee, tailor, 222 I.
Quong Act Tai & Co., groceries, and drugs, 200 I.
Quong Goon & Co., groceries, 224 I.
Quong Hing Lung & Co., groceries, 314 I.
Quong Hong Hi & Co., groceries, 414 I.
Quong Hop, wash house, e s 4th bet L and M.
Quong Kee, wash house, 415 12th.
Qung Song, wash house, 1617 3d.
Sam Chung, wash house, 724 L.
Sam Lee, wash house, n w cor 6th and L.
Sam Sing, wash house, 1025 5th.
Sam Wah, wash house, 1010 3rd.San Lung & Co., china goods, 526 J.
San Wah, wash house, 816 I.
Sang Hop, wash house 902 6th.
Sang Long, wash house 1425 Front.
Shun Leo, wash house, s s I bet Front and 2d.
Sing Chang, wash house 607 I.
Sing Hop wash house Ann bet Front and 2d. Wash'n
Sing Kee, wash house, 706 K.
Sing Wah, wash house 2d bet Ann and Harriet, Wash.
Sing Wah, wash house, 917 13th
Sing Yuen, wash house, 504 7th
Si Sing, wash house 1018 8th.
Son Sing, butcher shop, 412 I.
Son Wah, butcher, 308 I.
Sun Chung Kee & Co., groceries, 908 3rd.
Sun Tunk Wo, dry goods and notions., 321 I.
Sung Wo & Co., butchers and dealers in hogs, 315 I.
Tai Chung, groceries, 214 I.
Tai Jan, tailor, n s 1 bet 4th and 5th.
Tong Suck Hong, drug store, 230 I.
Tong Soong Tai, fruit and vegetables, 219 I.
TONG WO CHAN, importers Chinese goods, 300 I.
Ty Sing & Co., 302 I.
Uen Kee, wash house, 1010 6th.
Wah Hing & Co., groceries and drugs, 430 I.
Wah Kee, wash house, 912 5th.
Wah Lee, wash house 208 K.
Wah Lee & Co., butchers, 229½ I.
Wah Lun tailor. 410 I.
Wah Shung & Co., boots and shoes, 525 J.
Wing Sing, wash house, 306 K and 1003 K.
WO OWN YU KEE, wholesale groceries and provisions, 326 I.
Yee Chin Low, restaurant, 215 I
Yet Wo, tailor, 324 I.Yow Long, tailor, 212½ I.
Yow Long, tailor, 212 ½ I.
Yu Chung & Co., groceries, 320 I.

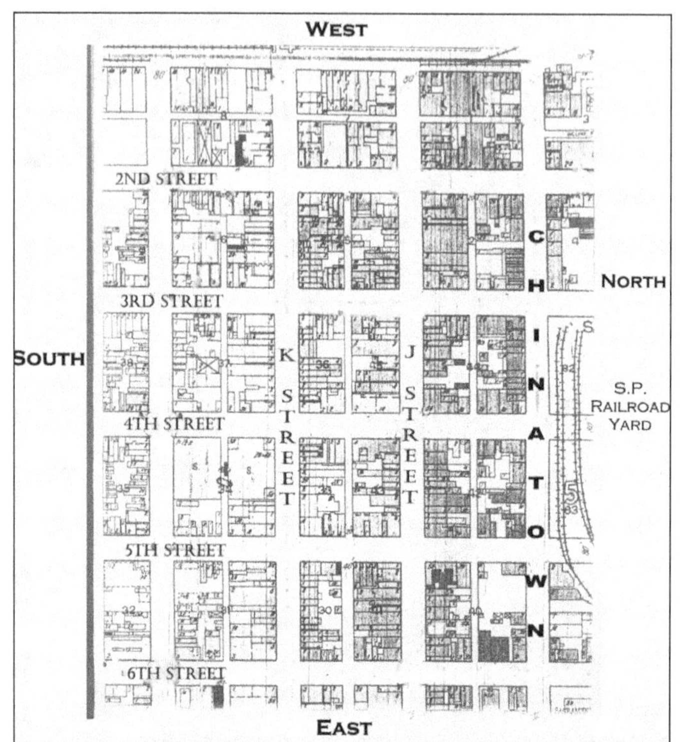

This is a map of Sacramento's Chinatown just south of the Southern Pacific Rail Yard in 1915. Chinatown was on I Street from Second Street to Sixth Street. Chinese residents referred to I street as Tong Yen Gai (Chinese Street).

This is the south side of I Street between Second and Third Streets in Chinatown. In the middle of the block is an herb store owned by S. Y. Wong. To the right of the herb store is Wing Fat Chong, a small grocery store owned by Louie Fat and Louie Wing. The picture was taken in the early 1940s. (Courtesy Ronald Lai and the Center for Sacramento History.)

Chun Jock Gee established the Tong Sun Company in the late 1800s, selling fish and produce wholesale. In the early 1900s, he started construction of a building for his business at 916–918 Third Street. The completed building is below. (Both, courtesy Dan Chan Jr.)

PARTNERSHIP LIST OF TONG SUNG CO.
SACRAMENTO, CALIF.

NO.	ACTIVE MEMBERS	NAME IN CHINESE	POSITION IN FIRM	AMOUNT OF INTEREST
1	CHAN TAI OY	陳帝鐳	MANAGER	$1,000.00
2	HEE FUK YUEN	許福元	BOOKKEEPER	1,000.00
3	LEONG CHONG LEE	梁璋利	SALESMAN	1,000.00
4	LEE TAI KING	李帝琼	BUYER	1,000.00
5	CHAN BING YUEN	陳炳元	SALESMAN	1,000.00
6	CHAN TAI YOUNG	陳帝鏞	MGR. RENO BRANCH	1,000.00
7	LEONG CHOCK CHONG	梁作鄺	SALESMAN	1,000.00
8	CHAN GIN CHEW	陳霑兆	SALESMAN	1,000.00
9	LEE QUONG CHUCK	李光灼	BOOKKEEPER	1,000.00
10	CHAN KUEI MEI	陳桂楣	IN CHINA	1,000.00
11	DING MON YEE	鄧文裕	IN CHINA	1,000.00
12	CHAN MON TONG	陳文通	IN CHINA	1,000.00
13	CHEN WING YEE	陳永裕	IN CHINA	1,000.00
14	SOON LUM TAI	孫林棣	IN CHINA	1,000.00
15	CHAN GIN FAI	陳霑輝	IN CHINA	1,000.00
16	CHAN HING	陳興	IN CHINA	1,000.00

STATE OF CALIFORNIA)
COUNTY OF SACRAMENTO) ss.

CHAN TAI OY, being first duly sworn deposes and says:

That he is a member of and partner in the firm of Tong Sung Co., a co-partnership; that affiant's position in said firm is "Manager"; that affiant prepared the foregoing partnership list and the same is true of his own knowledge.

IN WITNESS WHEREOF affiant has subscribed his name hereto this 8th day of May, 1930.

Chan Tai Oy
Affiant

Subscribed and sworn to before me this 8th day of May, 1930.

Donald E. Wachhorst
Notary Public in and for the County of Sacramento, State of California.

The Tong Sung Company initially had 10 partners. The firm was capitalized at $10,000. Later the number of partners increased to 16. This is the listing of the 16 partners in 1930. Chan Tai Oy became the managing partner in 1922 until 1933 when it closed due to the Depression. (Both, courtesy Dan Chan Jr.)

This is the delivery truck of the L. E. Chong and Company in the 1920s. Based at a farm in the Sacramento Delta, the company sold produce under the Bellhop Brand label. The Tong Sung Company in Sacramento received their produce from this company. Lee Chong, a partner of L. E. Chong and Company, was the brother-in-law of Chan Tai Oy, the managing partner of Tong Sung Company. (Courtesy Dan Chan Jr.)

Harry Y. Wong (Wong Wing Gim) was born in China and immigrated to America in 1921. He worked for the Sheu Fong Company (a poultry business) and became a partner in August 1930. Being a partner gave him merchant status, enabling him to bring his wife and daughter to America. (Courtesy Janet Wong Chan.)

This picture of the east side of Third Street between I and J Streets was taken in the early 1900s. This is before the second story was added to the Hong King Lum building to the left. (Courtesy California Historical Society FN-34381.)

This picture is the west side of Third Street between I and J Streets during the mid-1930s. Sang Wo Lung Company, a Chinese grocery store, was located at 912 Third Street. The General Produce and Fish Company that opened in 1933 was located at 916–918 Third Street, the same location as the previous Tong Sung Company. (Courtesy Dan Chan Jr.)

The General Produce Company was established in 1933 at 916 Third Street. It relocated to 200 North Sixteenth Street in 1934 in the building located at the back center of the picture above. Chan Tai Oy was the managing partner of the company. This picture of Chan Tai Oy with the abacus on his desk was taken in his Sixteenth Street office in 1948 at the General Produce Company. (Both, courtesy Dan Chan Jr.)

The W-O Pharmacy store (above) was at the southeast corner of Third and I Streets. Wilbert Wong was the pharmacist. He was the son of Sing Tao Wong, who immigrated to America in 1868. The Hong King Lum restaurant was located above the W-O Pharmacy, which operated during the 1930s. (Courtesy Frank L. Wong.)

T. Wah Hing (Yee Lok Sam) practiced herbal medicine at 725 J Street in Sacramento. He was the son of the well-known herbalist Yee Fan Cheung of Fiddletown. T. Wah Hing practiced herbal medicine in Sacramento before the 1900s, initially at 707 J Street. In 1905, Hing moved to 725 J Street, where he practiced for the next 30 years. (Courtesy Sylvia Sun Minnick.)

Bert Sui Fong (Fong Kwong Huan) immigrated to America as a student in 1910. He worked in various jobs until 1921 before he established the Sheu Fong Company, a poultry dealer at 420–422 I Street. Bert Sui Fong is on the right next to the Sheu Fong Company delivery truck, and Git Fong is on the left. This picture was taken in 1926. (Courtesy Robert H. W. Fong.)

In 1931, Bert Sui Fong remodeled the Sheu Fong Company building by adding a brick front. This picture was taken during the Fourth of July celebration in 1932 with the sales of fireworks in the front of the building. (Courtesy Merrily Fong Wong.)

Fannie Sing, born in 1897, and Hattie Sing, born in 1899, owned the Capital Letter Shop in Sacramento. Much of their business was composing and producing documents for the state legislature. The business in the 1920s was located in the Traveler's Hotel at Fifth and J Streets. They later moved to Thirtieth and O Streets and continued to operate until the 1950s. (Courtesy Art B. and Barbara Tom.)

This picture of Chinatown is the east side of Fourth Street between I and J Streets. Upstairs is the Bing Kong Tong Association. Downstairs to the right at the end of the building is a store owned by Quong Fung. The second door from the corner on the left is an herb store owned by Yick Sil Hong. The picture was taken in the 1950s. (Courtesy California Historical Society FN-34382.)

Gon Lip Wong (Mon Woey Wong) opened the First Peking Café on 917 Sixth Street in 1924. In the picture are his children in 1933. From left to right are (first row) Kay and Mamie; (second row) Frank, Fay, and Larry. Gon Lip operated at that location until the restaurant closed in 1936. He then moved the restaurant to 1114 Eighth Street and called it the New Peking Café, pictured below. In that picture are, from left to right, Mamie, Fay, and Frank. Subsequent to the New Peking Café, Gon Lip moved twice more, to 719 J Street and finally to 2900 Thirty-fifth Street. (Both, courtesy Frank L. Wong.)

This is the grand opening of the Sacramento's Farmer Market, a wholesale marketplace, on November 18, 1933. The market was south of Broadway between Third and Fifth Streets. Most of the distributors were Chinese Americans who farmed in Sacramento's outlying areas. (Both, courtesy Barry Lim.)

In the 1940s, Harry Y. Wong established the new Save-A-Lot Market on Stockton Boulevard and Fifth Avenue very close to the California State Fairgrounds on Stockton Boulevard and Broadway. Each year during state fair time, Harry looked forward to providing free parking to his many friends attending the fair.

Like many of the children of Chinese American families, Janet, the second-oldest daughter of Harry Y. Wong, is learning early to help in the family business. This picture was taken in the 1940s. (Courtesy Janet Wong Chan.)

The Sun Sun Café was located at 307–309 J Street. It was one of the four major Chinese restaurants in Chinatown. Louie Wing, owner of Sun Sun Café, was a chef at the Hong King Lum restaurant before leaving in 1934 to open his own restaurant. He was the executive chef at his restaurant and was known as "Head Chef Wing" (How Cheuih Wing) in the Chinese community. His specialty was fried whole chicken stuffed with sweet rice. Louie Wing is shown here checking on the family's holiday turkey in 1950. He operated the Sun Sun Café until late 1967 when redevelopment of the area began. (Above, courtesy Ronald Lai; left, courtesy Jim and Ruth Lowe.)

SPECIAL SUGGESTIONS

Roast Pork	.25
Fried Spare Ribs, Sweet and Sour Flavor	.45
Fried Spare Ribs with Pineapple	.50
Fried Spare Ribs with Black Bean Sauce	.40
Fried Spare Ribs with Chinese Cheese	.40
Minced Pork with Salted Eggs, Steamed	.25
Minced Pork with Leg of Salted Duck	.35
Pickled Green with Pork	.25
Green Pepper with Pork or Beef	.25
Green with Pork	.20
Bean Cake with Pork	.20
Minced Pork with Dry Oyster	.50
Chinese Sausage	.30
Ginger Beef	.30
Fried Salted Fish	.20
Minced Pork with Water Chestnut	.50
Fried Tripe	.40

SEA FOODS

Fresh Shrimp, Fried on Shell	.35
Fresh Shrimp Chop Suey	.65
Fried Fresh Shrimp with Tomato Sauce	.65
Fried Skinned Shrimps	.70
Bitter Melon with Shrimp	.65
Fresh Fish Chop Suey	.50
Fried Abalone	.50
Steamed Fish	.50

SPECIAL CHINESE DINNER

55c
Chinese Noodle
Fresh Shrimp Egg Foyoung
Pork Chow Mein
Rice Tea
Rice Cake

65c
Chicken Noodle Soup
Mushroom Chop Suey
Chicken Chow Mein
Rice Tea

80c
Chicken Mushroom Soup
Chicken Chop Suey with Tomato
Subgum Chow Mein with Almond
Rice Tea

SANDWICHES

Chicken Sandwich	.30
Cold Ham Sandwich	.30
Egg Sandwich	.15
Roast Pork Sandwich	.15
Fried Ham Sandwich	.15
Ham and Egg Sandwich	.20
Toast	.10

BEVERAGES

Soda Water
Wine
Beer
Whiskey

SUN SUN CAFE
307 J ST.
Sacramento, California
Phone: Dial 2-1637

Menu

Chow Mein and Noodles Specialty

ALL KINDS OF CHINESE DISHES TO TAKE HOME

Open 10:30 A. M. to 12 Midnight
10:30 A. M. to 2:00 A. M. Saturday

This is the English version of the menu for Sun Sun Café in the 1950s. Since Sacramento had a relatively large Chinese-speaking community, there was also a Chinese version of the menu available. Notice that an order of Greens with Pork (choy sum yuk) was just 20¢, and a Roast Pork sandwich was 15¢. (Both, courtesy Ronald Lai.)

CHINESE MENU

CHOW MEINS
(Fried or Crisp)

Fine Cut Pork Chow Mein	.40
Fine Cut Pork Chow Mein for 2	.75
Subgum Chow Mein, Single	.55
Subgum Chow Mein, for 2	1.00
Chicken Chow Mein	.50
Fine Cut Fresh Chicken Chow Mein, Extra Fine, Single	.65
Fine Cut Fresh Chicken Chow Mein, Extra Fine, for 2	1.20
Subgum Chicken Chow Mein, Single	.70
Subgum Chicken Chow Mein, for 2	1.25
Fine Cut Beef Chow Mein	.40
Fresh Shrimp Chow Mein	.45
Fresh Shrimp Chow Mein for 2	.80

NOODLES

Pork Noodle	.20
Chop Suey Noodle	.30
Chicken Noodle	.30
Duck Noodle	.30
Tomato and Curry Noodle	.30
Yee Foo Mein	1.00
Yee Foo Mein	.65
Young Chow Wor Mein	1.00
Young Chow Wor Mein	.65
Won Ton (Chinese Ravioli)	.20
Chop Suey Won Ton	.30
Duck Won Ton	.30
War Won Ton	1.00
War Won Ton	.65
Fried War Ton	.65

CHOP SUEYS

Plain Chop Suey	.30
Vegetable Chop Suey	.25
Water Chestnut Chop Suey	.50
Mushroom Chop Suey	.50
Chicken Livers and Giblets Chop Suey	.30
Chop Suey with Chicken	.40
Subgum Chop Suey with Almonds	.55

SOUP

Chicken Broth	.10
Chicken and Rice Soup	.15
Bean Cake Soup	.15

CHINESE MENU

Chicken and Noodle Soup	.15
Chicken Broth with Egg	.25
Green Soup	.20
Giblet Soup	.40
Water Lily Nut Soup	.65
Abalone Soup	.65
Grass Mushroom Soup	.45
Chicken and Mushroom Soup	.65
Chop Suey Soup	.40
Sea Weed Soup	.20

RICE

Fried Rice with Roast Pork	.30
Chicken Fried Rice	.45
Fresh Shredded Chicken Fried Rice	.55
Fresh Shrimp Fried Rice	.40
Crab Meat Fried Rice	.40
Subgum Fried Rice	.45
Rice Steamed with Chicken	.55
Rice Steamed with Chicken Boneless	.80
Rice Steamed with Beef	.35
Plain Rice	.10

POULTRY SELECTIONS

Chicken Chop Suey	.75
Extra Fine Cut Chicken Chop Suey	1.25
Chicken with Pineapple	1.25
Chicken with Tomato	.75
Chicken with Chinese Green	1.25
Almond Chicken, Dice Cut	1.25
Cho Koo Gai Kell (Ball Chicken Fried)	1.25
Downe Koo Woot Gai Roast Chicken, With Black Mushroom	1.25
Steamed Chicken with Mushroom	1.25
Fried Chicken	.75
Fried Squab with Spiced Salt, Each	
Roast Duck	.50
Wo Su Op (Duck Cooked in Canton Style)	1.25

EGGS IN ORIENTAL FASHION

Plain Egg Foyoung	.35
Chicken Egg Foyoung	.45
Fresh Shrimp Egg Foyoung	.45
Crab Meat Egg Foyoung	.45
Roast Pork and Egg, Canton Style	.40
Fresh Shrimp with Egg	.40

This is a picture of the south side of I Street between Fourth and Fifth Streets. In the 1920s, a friend offered Bert Sui Fong and his wife the vacant building on the left, 420–422 I Street, where they started the Sheu Fong Company, a poultry business. (Courtesy Robert W. H. Fong.)

The Hong King Lum Café was opened in 1906 by Dong Haw, Dong Oy Lung, and Dong Bock Lung. It was one of the largest Chinese restaurants in Chinatown. In 1911, Dong Haw opened Yick Chong Company below the restaurant. It was later called S. P. Depot Market. (Courtesy Sylvia Sun Minnick.)

Harry Y. Wong with his brother, David Wing, opened the China Star restaurant at 3011 Broadway. The grand opening on February 3, 1950, was celebrated with much fanfare. The restaurant served both Chinese and American cuisine and provided employment opportunities for many of the family's relatives from China. All of Harry Wong's children worked at the restaurant, from cleaning up to being hostesses and cashier. (Courtesy Janet Wong Chan.)

In 1939, Frank Fat (Dong Sai Fat) purchased the Truckadero restaurant at 806 L Street, which became Frank Fat's Chinese restaurant. The restaurant was very successful and was known as a place where politicians and lobbyists gathered. It became legendary as California's "Third House of the Legislature," where landmark bills were drafted in back booths and tort reform arose out of a famous "napkin" deal.

Bill Wong, born in Taishan, China, came to America in 1922. He grew up on a farm in Penryn and later worked and owned several grocery stores. With his parents and siblings, he opened the first Bel Air Market in 1955 at 6231 Fruitridge Road. Eventually they expanded to 18 Bel Air Markets before selling the stores to Raley's in 1992. He is shown here taking delivery of produce at General Produce Company in the late 1930s. (Both, courtesy Dan Chan Jr.)

Many of the Chinese families lived in Chinatown or south of M Street (Capitol Avenue) prior to the mid-1950s. This is the home of Sam Fong's family on N Street between Fourth and Fifth Streets in Sacramento. This picture was taken in the 1930s. (Courtesy Roger G. F. Fong.)

This is the east side of Fifth Street between M and N Streets. Seen here from left to right are the homes of the Ray Kwong family, the Fong Sik family, and the Fong Tune family. This picture was taken in the 1940s. (Courtesy Merrily Fong Wong.)

This was the home of Bert Shue Fong's family. He was the owner of the Sheu Fong Company, a poultry market in Chinatown. The home was located on the west side of Fourth at 1416 Fourth Street. In this 1926 photograph, Bert Fong is standing on the running board, and Floyd Fong is in the driver's seat. (Courtesy Robert W. H. Fong.)

This was the residence of the Lai family. It was on the east side of Fifth Street between M and N Streets. The garage below was converted into the Dun-Rite Shoe Repair Shop, operated by Gee Lai. The residence to the right belonged to George Au's family. This picture was taken in the 1940s. (Courtesy Ronald Lai and Center for Sacramento History.)

Three

THE PIONEER CHINESE FAMILIES OF SACRAMENTO

During the Gold Rush, California was a wild and lawless place, attracting a primarily male population. Because of the immensity of the gold deposits, the state developed quickly and soon women joined the gold miners—all except for the Chinese. Their experience was different. Rather than finding in California a free and open land, the Chinese encountered racism and legal discrimination, which meant that for them, California would remain a lawless land for many decades to come. The most devastating blow to the Chinese came from the California State Supreme Court decision in 1854 that held the Chinese could not testify in court. In the *People v. Hall* case, three Chinese witnesses were called to testify against the murderer of a Chinese person. A conviction was secured, and the defendant appealed. The California Supreme Court overturned the conviction, holding that the Chinese witnesses should not have been allowed to testify. The court ordered the convicted murderer freed. Thus the Chinese were denied protection under American law. European Americans could assault, even kill Chinese Americans without fear of punishment in California. Then the Chinese Exclusion Act was passed, strictly limiting the entry of Chinese to this country. The law was bad enough. Worse, Chinese Americans could not rely on the fair administration of the law. In the first decade after the passage of the act, Chinese Americans filed 7,000 appeals in federal court against the immigration service. In the vast majority of these cases, Chinese petitioners prevailed. Such a record of losses by the authorities, denying entry to Chinese immigrants knowing the courts would overrule their decision, amounted to an abuse of power. But immigration officials persisted, following an unspoken government policy of discouraging the formation of Chinese families in America. The cumulative effect of this legal discrimination delayed the start of first true American-born Chinese generation by more than 50 years. When legal discrimination against the Chinese declined and starting families became safer, Chinese Americans in Sacramento were in the vanguard of this development. Chinese Americans had always considered Sacramento a friendly town and a good place to raise a family. By moving outside Chinatown several decades before Chinese Americans in San Francisco's Chinatown, they integrated their families into a more American lifestyle. That trend continues today.

Yee Hing Chow (Yuen Chow) was born in the 1870s. He came to America in 1880. He was a prospector and worked on constructing railroads. He settled in Sacramento and later returned to China. (Courtesy Eva Chow Fong, Ed.D.)

Sing Tao Wong (Wong Kue Ngon) was born in 1841 in China. He came to America in 1868 and married Shee Chin around 1893. He had three sons and eight daughters. He owned a grocery store on Third Street between I and J Streets in Sacramento's Chinatown. This is a picture of his family taken in 1917. (Courtesy Frank L. Wong.)

This is a picture of Wong Leong Gak with his wife in the late 1920s. He owned one of the four major Chinese restaurants in Chinatown. His restaurant was called the China Republic Restaurant (Chung Kuo Lau) and was located at 921–923 Third Street. (Courtesy Sylvia Sun Minnick.)

This early 1920s picture shows Bert Sui Fong, seated, with his wife, Suey Sum Yee Fong, and Bert's cousin. Bert established the Sheu Fong Poultry Company in 1921. Over the years, the company grew to become the largest poultry establishment in Sacramento County, supplying many hotels, restaurants, and even casinos in Reno. (Courtesy Robert W. H. Fong.)

Frank Fat (Dong Sai Fat) was born in 1904 in Taishan. He came to America in 1919. In 1924, he returned to China and married Yee Lai-Ching (Mary). He returned to America in 1926 and 10 years later brought over his wife and son. He subsequently had five more children. (Courtesy Fat Family Collection, California State University, Sacramento Special Collection and University Archives.)

Gon Yee Fong was born in China. She married Wee Fong in 1913 and later came to America and settled in Sacramento. Her husband, Wee Fong, was the nephew of Fong Sik and worked at the State Market on Sixth and M Streets. This picture was taken in 1913. (Courtesy Betty Chan Fong.)

Kum York Auyoung was born in China and married Young Lee. She and her husband settled in Sacramento in 1923. This picture was taken when she was a student in China in the early 1920s. (Courtesy Betty Lee Mar.)

Bessie Wong was the daughter of Sing Tao Wong and Chin Shee. She was born in 1896 in Sacramento. She married Lim Non Yue, a farmer. The picture was taken in 1920. (Courtesy Frank L. Wong.)

Shee Leong Chong, center, was born in China in 1871. She came to America in 1889 and settled in Sacramento in 1941. She is considered the matriarch of the Leong Chong family and is known by many as Grandma Leong Yee Chong. This is a picture of her *dai sangyaht* (big birthday) with her family members in 1922. She passed away in 1958 at the age of 87. (Courtesy Dan Chan Jr.)

John Sing, the son of Chan Sing and Lillie Lee, was born in 1885 in Sacramento. He married Cheong Yee in 1922. He owned and farmed in Sutter Basin, West Sacramento, North Natomas, and the land now occupied by Sacramento State University. He raised corn, wheat, safflower, and sugar beets. In the 1924 picture is John Sing, Cheong Yee, and John Sing Jr. (Courtesy Art B. and Barbara Tom.)

These three women are dressed to party. They are, from left to right, Mrs. Chan Kong Sun, Mrs. Suey Chan Wong, and Cheong Yee Sing, who was married to John Sing. This picture was taken in 1925. (Courtesy Frank L. Wong.)

Yee Shai Wun was born in 1911 in Dai Hong Village near Guangzhou, China. Her father, Yee Check Lai, was a good friend of Dr. Sun Yat-sen and worked for him in his administration. Yee Shai Wun married Harry Y. Wong in 1929 and settled in Sacramento in 1935. This picture was taken in 1929 in China. (Courtesy Janet Wong Chan.)

Rose Luke arrived in Sacramento as the bride of Chan Tai Young (Carl Y. Chan). She was known in Chinatown as "Dai Yat Leang" ("No. 1 Beauty"). She was the granddaughter of Lu Hao Tung, the second-in-command to Dr. Sun Yat-sen during China's Revolution and later the first revolutionary martyr of the Republic of China. This picture was taken in the 1930s. (Courtesy Betty Chan Fong.)

Quan Y. Luke was born in China and settled in Sacramento in 1941. He was the grandson of Lu Hao-tung, second-in-command to Dr. Sun Yat-sen during China's Revolution. He was a veteran of World War II and after the war worked at the Sacramento Army Depot. Luke (right) is shown with his sister Rose and her husband, Carl Chan (left), in 1941. (Courtesy Roger G. F. and Florence Fong.)

Young Lee was born in Hawaii in 1897. He married Kum York Auyoung, and they made Sacramento their home in 1923. He was a fruit and vegetables distributor to restaurants and hotels in Sacramento. They had three daughters and four sons. Three of the sons entered the military and were decorated war heroes. The above family picture was taken in 1937. (Courtesy Betty Lee Mar.)

Mary Fat (Yee Lai Ching) was born in China. She married Frank Fat in 1924 in China but did not join him in America until 1936. Here she is with her son Wing Kai and daughter Jean in 1938 at Capitol Park. (Courtesy Jean Fat Lai.)

William Yue Fong was born in China in 1899 and arrived in America as a teenager. He returned to China and married Lee Sui Ang in 1920. He returned to America by himself. Lee Siu Ping joined him in Sacramento in 1937. They had four girls and four boys. This picture was taken in China in 1920. (Courtesy Eva Chow Fong, Ed.D.)

From left to right are Mrs. Chan Lee, Mrs. Leong, and Mrs. Gee Lai in 1929. Mrs. Leong and Mrs. Lai lived in neighboring villages in China and both came to America on the SS *President Cleveland* in 1924. Mrs. Leong was the wife of Leong Chung Hee, the owner of Leong Fish Market on Third Street between I and J Streets in the 1940s. (Courtesy Ronald Lai.)

Joseph Yee was born in China. In 1916, at the age of 16, he immigrated to America. He worked the gold mines in the Sierras and eventually moved to Sacramento. He married Rose Mae Lee in 1929. Rose was born in Sacramento, graduating from Sacramento High School. They started their first grocery store at Eleventh and Q Streets in 1936 and later several other markets. In the mid-1950s, they opened Grand View Market on Fiftieth Street and Folsom Boulevard, one of the first supermarkets in Sacramento. The Chinese American Council of Sacramento Hall of Fame Honorees was awarded posthumously to Joseph and Rose Yee in 2006. (Courtesy Kari Yee.)

Jang Quin, above, came to America in the 1910s. He settled in Sacramento in 1931 and opened the Young China restaurant on Thirty-fifth Street in Oak Park. In 1947, he moved his restaurant to 913 Third Street in Chinatown. He operated this restaurant until he retired in 1957. He is shown in 1931 with his wife, Dora. (Courtesy Mary Tom.)

Wanda Fong (Ng Yok Woon) was born in China. She came to America in 1942 at the age of 13. She married Gary Fong and moved to Sacramento. At right, she is shown with her mother, Wong Fay Gen, in 1940. (Courtesy Wanda Fong.)

During World War II, there was a labor shortage in the California state government. To solve this problem, the state recruited seniors from Sacramento High School for the key-punch work program. The students received pay and received school credits at the same time. Ruby Lai (left) and Margaret Fong (right) were part of that program working at the State Department of Employment on Tenth and P Streets. (Courtesy Ruby Lee.)

Gee Lem and his wife started the Golden West Grocery Store (below) in 1939 on Main and Davis Streets in Vacaville. Gee Lem lived in Sacramento but commuted every day to Vacaville to manage the grocery store. In 1948, he moved the store across the street and continued operating it until the early 1960s. (Courtesy Robert W. H. Fong.)

Harry Y. Wong periodically would have his family picture taken by the fountain near the State Capitol Building. Five of his children entered the medical profession: Gordon and Wardon as medical doctors, Janet and Julie as dentists, and Eleanor as an optometrist. Shown here from left to right are Eleanor, Sylvia, Wardon, Gordon, Julie, Janet, Lily, Yee Sai Wun, and Harry Y. Wong. This picture was taken in 1949. (Courtesy Janet Wong Chan.)

Louie Wing immigrated to America in 1920. He worked at the Hong King Lum restaurant until 1934 and then opened the Sun Sun Café at 307 J Street. Here is his family in 1948. From left to right, they are (first row) Clara, Sally, Ruth with son Mark, and Mrs. Louie Wing; (second row) Henry, Jim Lowe (son-in-law), Louie Wing, and John. (Courtesy Dr. William Henry Chan.)

Herbert Gee was born in Oroville. He graduated from the University of California at Berkeley in 1935 with a degree in engineering. He settled in Sacramento and was a civil engineer for the Division of Highways (Caltrans), Bridge Department for 33 years. He retired in 1968. He is shown with his wife, Ada Look; Marilyn; and Malcolm in 1946. (Courtesy Ada Gee.)

Louie Wey King (Louie Him Yuey) entered America as a merchant in 1925. He owned Louie's Meat Market at Fifth and J Streets from 1932 to the 1950s until redevelopment forced the closure of his business. He then opened Louie's Market at Twentieth and J Streets until he retired in the late 1960s. He is shown with his wife, granddaughter Christine, and son Walter in the 1950s. (Courtesy Easter Jang.)

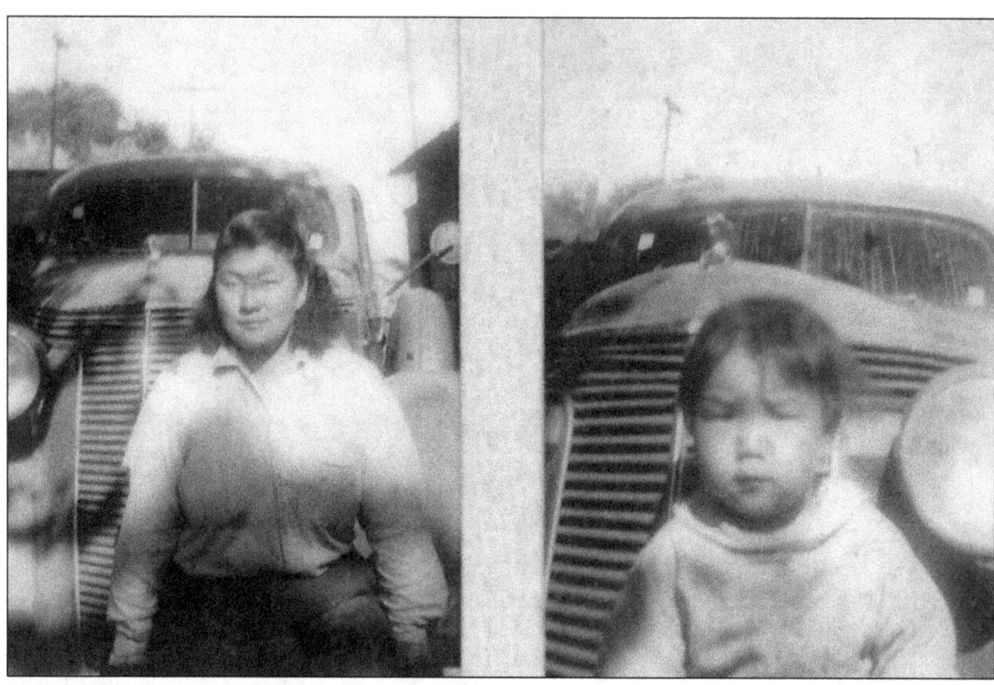

HEADQUARTERS WESTERN DEFENSE COMMAND AND FOURTH ARMY
OFFICE OF THE COMMANDING GENERAL
PRESIDIO OF SAN FRANCISCO, CALIFORNIA

TO ALL PERSONS CONCERNED:

The bearer of this permit is Shea Lim, a person of Japanese ancestry as to whom the provisions of the proclamations, exclusion orders and Civilian Restrictive Order No. 1 (Headquarters, Western Defense Command and Fourth Army) are hereby suspended.

This permit is good until revoked, and shall not be altered, copied, defaced or transferred.

By command of Lt. General DeWITT:

HUGH T. FULLERTON
Captain, A. G. D.
Assistant Adjutant General

HEADQUARTERS WESTERN DEFENSE COMMAND AND FOURTH ARMY
OFFICE OF THE COMMANDING GENERAL
PRESIDIO OF SAN FRANCISCO, CALIFORNIA

TO ALL PERSONS CONCERNED:

The bearer of this permit is Virginia Lim, a person of Japanese ancestry as to whom the provisions of the proclamations, exclusion orders and Civilian Restrictive Order No. 1 (Headquarters, Western Defense Command and Fourth Army) are hereby suspended.

This permit is good until revoked, and shall not be altered, copied, defaced or transferred.

By command of Lt. General DeWITT:

HUGH T. FULLERTON
Captain, A. G. D.
Assistant Adjutant General

After the start of World War II in 1942, Pres. Franklin Delano Roosevelt signed Executive Order 9066, which required persons of Japanese ancestry to relocate to internment camps. Shea, a Japanese woman, and her children were required to relocate even though she was married to Yue Lim, a Chinese man. They hired an attorney and secured a last-minute order that provided an exemption with identification cards to Shea and her four children. Since her husband, Yue Lim, operated a farm in the Pocket area of Sacramento, Shea and the children were considered under house arrest and could not leave the farm without the identification cards and an official escort. These were the front and back of the identification cards of Shea and her daughter, Virginia. (Both, courtesy Virginia Lim Hashisaka.)

Yue Lim (Lim Gon Yue) was born in China. He emigrated to Mexico and eventually settled in Sacramento in the early 1930s. He was a truck farmer in the Pocket area of Sacramento. The picture was taken in the late 1930s. (Courtesy Virginia Lim Hashisaka.)

This is a picture of Yue Lim's family. From left to right are (first row) Robert; Barry; Shea, wife of Yue Lim; Virginia; Yue Lim; and Henry; (second row) John Lim, a nephew that Yue Lim sponsored to America in 1944. This picture was taken in 1946. (Courtesy Virginia Lim Hashisaka.)

John Sing and Cheong Yee Sing hosted a party to welcome a school principal and her daughter from China. The party was held at John and Cheong's house in 1950. Attending the party from left to right are (seated) John Sing Sr. and Cheong Yee Sing; (standing) Beatrice Sing, unidentified, Wah Sim, Mary Fat, unidentified school principal, Song Moo and Carol Sing Tom. (Courtesy Art B. and Barbara Sing Tom.)

Chan Tai Oy immigrated to America in 1905. He married Tung Lin Leong in 1912. He worked for the Tong Sung Company. After it closed, he started General Produce Company. Here he is with his family in 1949. From left to right are (first row) Tung Lin Leong, Chan Tai Oy, Tom, Mavis (baby), and Mae; (second row) Kitty, Dan, Davis Sun (a nephew), Eddie, Mae, and Marjorie. (Courtesy Dan Chan Jr.)

Wong Yit Ying was born in 1904 in China. She married Chow Chew in 1921 and came to America in 1937. They settled in Sacramento in 1958. (Courtesy Eva Chow Fong, Ed.D.)

Howard Louie (Gin H. Yim) immigrated to America in 1941 from China. After serving in the army during World War II, he worked as a meat cutter. He is married to Suey J. Lee and has six children. From left to right are (first row) Easter, Edna, Hayworth (baby), and May; (second row) Christine, Suey, and Howard; (third row) Benny, a nephew. A daughter, Kam, remained in China. (Courtesy Easter Jang.)

Suey Sum Yee Fong, wife of Bert Fong, was born in 1892. In 1992, her two sons, Yen W. Fong and Robert W. H. Fong and their families gave a party to celebrate their mother's 100th birthday. The party was held at Hoi Sing Restaurant. (Courtesy Robert W. H. Fong.)

Helen Fong was born in Sacramento. Her father was Chuck Fong, a bodyguard for Sun Yet-sen. She married dentist Hing Owyang Jr., and they had three children. All three of their children are in the medical profession: Deborah and Greg are dentists, following in their father's profession, and Elizabeth is a physician. Deborah, at the age of six, was the first Chinese American to win the Grand National Twirling championship in 1981. (Courtesy Helen Owyang.)

Four

The Sacramento Chinese American Community

As the Chinese brought their wives and children to America after the turn of the 20th century, the community changed. Some of the male entertainment businesses relocated to the newly built Chinatowns in the Sacramento Delta. The community within Sacramento became more family oriented. Churches had been an important part of the community since the founding of the Chinese Baptist Church in 1854. Other churches soon followed and remain an active part of the community today. Family associations also played an important role in the community. In the 1920s, Chinese American families moved to the neighborhood south of Chinatown to live in houses and surroundings more suitable for family life. Almost all of their children went to nearby Lincoln School. Many Sacramento Chinese Americans made lifelong friends at this school. An active alumni group, unusual for a public school, exists even today. As the population of young Chinese Americans increased, new organizations formed to meet their needs. First among them were Chinese schools teaching language and history from the homeland. Chung Wah Chinese School was founded in 1908, Kwai Wah School in the 1920s. A girls' club called the Wah Keong Club was active in the 1930s. The YWCA sponsored a girl's club called the Wah Lungs in the 1940s. The boys had their own club called the Wah Yens. At Sacramento High School, the Chinese Student Club became an important club at the school more than 50 years ago. By the 1950s, with the number of Chinese American students significant at the local city college, students formed the Jai Sei Chi as a social club. Chinese American students in Sacramento were also active in sports, forming baseball and basketball teams that played in leagues against other city teams or teams from other Chinatowns. Drum and bugle corps were also very popular. The first one was at the Chung Wah Chinese School. Later the Capitol Lions Club sponsored a Boy Scout drum and bugle corps. The Mandarin Drum and Bugle Corps, started in the 1960s, was invited to play in Taiwan during Chiang Kai-shek's inauguration. Today Chinese Americans have assimilated into all neighborhoods and professions in Sacramento and are represented in local politics.

The Kwai Wah Church was founded in 1924 at Fifth and P Streets. From left to right, the founding members seen here are (first row) Mrs. Kwok, Mrs. Lum, Mrs. Smith, Mrs. Fong Sik, Mrs. Kwong, and Mrs. Sunny Fong; (second row) Sunny Fong, Ed W. Smith, Fong Sik, Fong Jong, Gain Foon Fong, and Rev. W. S. Kwok. (Courtesy Merrily Fong Wong.)

The Wonder Years: 1927—1944
at Kwai Wah Chinese Language School

Au Family
Henry, Edward, May

Chan, Qi Family
Eddie, Tommy, Daniel, Margie

Chan Family
Edmund, Bun Su, Betty, Doris Jenny

Chan, Joe

Chan, Shack Lee Family
Loretta, Elmer, Edna, Rose

Chinn, Net Family
Franklin, Florence, Leland, Allen, Holland

Chow Family
William, Roslie, Georgiana

Chung, Roger

Dong Family
James, Ella, Evelyn, Laura

Fat, Frank Family
Joe Get, Wing Kai

Fong, Dennis

Fong, Fu Family
Richard, Rose, Priscilla

Fong, Gay Sou Family
William, Edward, Audrey, Violet, Roger

Fong, Harold

Fong, Hui Family
Logan, Soo Kee, Virginia, Rose, Violet, Harry, Henry, Kui, James

Fong, Joe Fu Family
Joe, Jack, Bobbie, Bernie, Mary, Helen

Fong, Kong Ngan Family
Molly, Hoover, William, Violet, Dorothy, Heddy, Edward

Fong, Liang Gong Family
Ednamae, Edmund, Evan, Edward, Pearl

Fong, Man Mou Family
Carl, Ben, Frank, May

Fong, Sam Family
Jerold, Harold, Sylvia, Keith, Cuny

Fong, Sik Family
Ann, Lawerence, Mary, Raymond

Fong, Siu Sou Family
Henry, Jeannette, Annamae

Fong, Wei Family
Charles, Russell, Dorothy, Hellen, Allen

Fong, Wing Sou Family
Sooky, Dora, Lilly

Fong, Yan Family
William, Bill, May, Tuey, Velma, Penny, Gon, Kim

Fong, York

Fong Family
Edgar, Edward Stu

Fong Family
George, Henry, Anna, Anita, Margaret, Gladys

Fong Family
Gladys, Joe, Soon, Sylvia

Fong Family
Hong, Sandr

Fong Family
Mildred, John, Kenneth

Gee, Alvin

Hue, Marshall Family
Alice, Frank, Agnes, Larry

Hue, Sui Sing Family
Leland, Rena, May, Edna, Connie

Jan Family
David, Robert, Daisy

Joe Family
Harry, Fannie, Rose, Willie

Kwok, Wai Sing Family
Johnny, Andrew, Alice, Sara, Esther

Kwong, Pak Ming Family
May, Marilyn, Ruby, Leonard, Raymond

Kwong, Sou Ho Family
Grace, Johnny, Ella, Jimmy

Kwong Family
Sunny, Eugene

Lai Family
Johnny, Ruby, Jimmy, Henry

Leong Family
Evan, Harold

Leong Family
Hebert, Evelyn, Richard, Peter

Louie, Kam Chuen Family
Jack, William, Fee, Jan, Charlie, May

Louis Family
Lookie, Danny, David, Edna

Lowe Family
Baron, Edgar

Lum, Jack

Lum, Thorton

Pang Family
Mona, Andrew, Henry, Bobbie

Sing Family
John, Gloria

Wong, Sam Family
Laura, Edward, Norma, LaBelle, Merle, Diane, Arvilla, Elaine

Yee Family
Jack, Betty

Yee Family
George, Donald, Harold Fem, Grace

You, Dora

This is a listing of the families and friends at the Kwai Wah Chinese Language School from 1927 to 1944, compiled by Ellen Kwong. Ellen referred to the period as the "wonder years." (Courtesy Joe S. Fong.)

This is the 1927 graduation class of Kwai Wah School. Pictured from left to right are (first row) William Wong, Bob Jang, Delores Kwong Mock, Edith Wong, Mae Hue Wong, Poy Kwong, and Evan Leong; (second row) Gin Fong, Chuck Fong, Dan Chan, Albert ?, George Wong, Joseph Kwong, and Woodrow Jang; (third row) Fong Shew Sing, unidentified, Fong Sik, unidentified, Rev Kwok, and Mrs. Kwok. (Courtesy Joe S. Fong.)

The Chinese Methodist Church, Mee Wah, was located at 1413 Sixth Street from 1926 to 1960. During redevelopment of the area, the church moved to its present location at 2470 Twenty-eighth Avenue. This 1930s picture features the church's members and the church's minister, Hiram Fong, who stands at far right. (Courtesy Merrily Fong Wong.)

The ministry of the present Chinese Community Church began in 1924. It was initially called the Kwai Wah Chinese Language School and held classes in a residence on Fifth and P Streets. It

later moved to 519 N Street. The church moved once more in 1951 to its present location at 5600 Gilgunn Way. This picture is at the N Street building in 1938. (Courtesy Merrily Fong Wong.)

HISTORY OF THE FIRST
CHINESE BAPTIST CHURCH

1854 Rev. J. Lewis Shuck, first American Baptist missionary to China, sent by the Southern Baptist Board to the Pacific Coast to work among the Chinese, began his work in Sacramento.
1855 Chinese chapel erected on 6th and H Streets and dedicated on June 10, 1855.
1860 Chinese Baptist Church organized in January 1860 by fifteen members of the First Baptist Church with Rev. J. Lewis Shuck as pastor.
1888 Miss Eliza Willsie, under appointment of the Women's Baptist Home Mission Society, founded the Chinese Baptist Mission.
Visitation, Sunday Evening worship service and English night school ministries began.
1917 Mrs. Mary Allen, commissioned by the Women's American Baptist Home Mission Board, organized the Chinese Baptist Mission Sunday School.
1920 Rev. Yee Sur Wun, first Chinese pastor called from Canton, China.
Mrs. Rachel Yuke started a Chinese Language School at the Mission. The Baptist, Congregational, and Methodist Chinese missions started monthly Union Sunday worship services at the various facilities.
1923 Mrs. E. E. (Maude)Pook, a voluntary worker from the First Baptist Church became the Mission superintendent and started the first Vacation Bible School.
Craft training begun for young men by Mrs. Pook.
1926 Chinese Baptist Mission moves to 525 M Street. First location away from Chinatown.
1930 Rev. Lee Shau Yan, Chinese pastor called from Canton, China.
1934 The Northern California Baptist Convention purchased the building at 421 M Street on February 26, 1934 for $3,250. The funds were partly raised by the Mission members and many Chinese communities. Third floor rooms were rented out to newly-arrived young men from China.
1944 Chinese Baptist Mission moves to the Lincoln Christian Center at the request of the Baptist Convention.
1946 Rev. Paul Fong called to be pastor of the church and served until 1948.
1947 Miss Mary Opal Crone, under appointment of the Women's American Baptist Home Mission Society began leadership with the Sunday School Center.
1949 Miss Eleanor V. Crone, under appointment of the Women's American Baptist Home Mission Society began service with the Chinese Baptist Mission and the Locke Christian Center.
Youth fellowship organized.
1952 During Miss Eleanor Crone's time of service, the First Chinese Baptist Church was organized on October 14, 1952 with 46 charter members.
Women's Bible study group and Adult choir organized.
1954 100th anniversary of Baptist ministry among the West Coast Chinese was celebrated.
1955 Baptist Ladies Fellowship Guild organized (later became American Baptist Women).
1956 Morning worship services initiated in place of the evening service.
1958 Thursday night prayer meetings began.
1959 The present building at 4470 Custis was purchased for $30,000 on September 15.
1960 The official dedication of the church building on January 24, 1960.
1966 Alterations in the church building, including a new baptistry, were dedicated on March 27. On the same day, the interim pastor, Rev. Dwight S. Coad was installed as pastor.
1968 Rev. Donald W. Jee was installed as pastor on December 15. He was the first Chinese-American pastor of our church.
1970 Air-conditioning system installed in the sanctuary by the men of our church.
1971 The evangelistic musical "What's It All About, Anyhow?" was presented on tour directed by Adele Nishimura and Linda Thengvall. Adults and youth from several different churches participated in this effort.
1972 Richard Palone was called as our first youth director for expanding the ministry to high-schoolers and college students. The youth fellowship acquired the name "Sonseekers".
The loans on the church property and air-conditioning system were paid off.
1977 Many church members participated in the "I Found It" campaign coordinated by Campus Crusade for Christ among Sacramento churches.
Led by Choir Directors, George and Florence Sholin, our church choir traveled to Hawaii for the Chinese Christian Confab Conference, ministering in music at several homes, missions and churches.
Church building project completed in which the sanctuary and Crone Hall were connected.
1981 Russell Moy called as the church's second pastor.
1984 Pastor Moy is ordained by the church on June 10.

The Chinese Baptist Church is the first Chinese church in the Sacramento area. It was established in 1855 at Sixth and H Streets. It moved several more times before purchasing a building at 4470 Custis Avenue in 1959 for $30,000. (Courtesy Joe S. Fong.)

This is the Chinese Baptist Mission Church choir at 528 N Street in 1932. From left to right are (first row) Mabel Fong, M. Yuke, Lily Fong, unidentified, Lily Fong, and Laura Dong; (second row) director Rachel Joe Yuke, Ella Dong, Lucy Fong, Helen Chan, pianist Ruby Yuke, Rosie May Fong, Matida Chan, and Rev. Lee Shaw Yan, pastor; (third row) Benjamin Yuke, Jim Fong, and Paul Yuke. (Courtesy Joe S. Fong.)

The Chinese School, Chung Wah, was founded in 1908 in Sacramento at 218 I Street. After a year, it moved to 915 Third Street. In 1931, the school moved to 522 M Street. In 1935, the school was incorporated as the Confucius Church of Sacramento and operated under the sponsorship of the Chinese Benevolent Association. (Courtesy Sylvia Sun Minnick.)

During the weekdays, the Chinese American children attended public school during the day and Chung Wah Chinese School in the evening. The Chinese school ran from 5:00 p.m. to 7:00 p.m. Saturday classes were from 9:00 a.m. to noon. This is the classroom at 522 M Street, shown in the early 1940s. (Courtesy Sally Chan Kan.)

The New Life Movement was created in February 1934 by Chiang Kai-shek and his wife, Soong May-ling. This picture was taken in front of the Chung Wah Chinese School at 522 M Street after the organizing ceremony of the New Life Movement in Sacramento. (Courtesy Betty Chan Fong.)

This is the graduating class (seventh term) at the Chung Wah Chinese School at 522 M Street. The two teachers are in the first row, on the left is John Lewis Fong and on the right is Yee Chew Nam. Yee Chun Po, the school principal, is in the back row, second from the left. This picture was taken in 1932. (Courtesy Roger W. H. Fong.)

This photograph of the Wah Keong Club on November 9, 1930, was taken at William Land Park. It was a Sacramento Chinese American girls' club. The girls are from left to right Florence Wong, two unidentified girls, Dorothy Lim, an unidentified girl, Nellie Dong, an unidentified girl, and Violet Wong. (Courtesy Frank L. Wong.)

The YWCA in the early 1940s sponsored a Sacramento Chinese America girls' club called the Wah Lungs. They held their fifth annual China Relief Dance on September 7, 1946, at Turn Verein Hall. All the officers of Wah Lungs are in the front row. The girls in the front from left to right are Evelyn Fong, Margaret Chan, Ruby Yien, Anna Ong, Mamie Wong, and Lillie Yee. (Courtesy Betty Chan Fong.)

These are the Wah Lung officers for 1949 and 1950. Betty Chan was elected president. From left to right are (seated) Betty Chan and Jessie Wong; (standing) Sally Yee, Jeannette Jung, Carol Jan, Joyce Tom, Patsy Yen, Florence Chan, and Sally Chan. (Courtesy Sally Chan Kan.)

The Wah Lungs held dances once a month on Friday nights. The dances were called the Rhythm Hour and were held at the YWCA at Seventeenth and K Streets in Sacramento. This is one of the dances held in 1949. (Courtesy Robert W. H. Fong.)

The Wah Lungs had their 13th annual September Dance in 1954 at the Senator Hotel. The theme that year was "The King and I." From left to right are (first row) Lily Fong, Eilen Fong, Barbara Fong, Mae Quan, and Joanne Lai; (second row) Jeanette Leong, Lori Lai, Marilyn Gee, Rhoda Yee, Betty You, Alice Fong, Beverly Dere, and Jean Fat. (Courtesy Betty Chan Fong.)

These were the Wah Lungs in 1958. Virginia Lim was the president that year. In the picture from left to right are (first row) Diana Tang, Vicki Lew, Judy Wong, Anna Fong, and Mary Ann Gee; (second row) Vicki Chan, Carlyn Wong, Beauty Yee, Virginia Lim, and Carol Mizutani; (third row) Betty Wong, Eva Chow, Sandra Wong, Cynthia Wong, Brenda Mar, and Joan Lee. (Courtesy Eva Chow Fong, Ed.D.)

17
16
8
7
6
1
5
3
2
4
19
20

A bazaar for raising funds was held at the Chung Wah Chinese School at 522 M Street in September 1946. In the picture, identified by a number at the event, are (1) Frank Wong, (2) Willie Yee, (3) Joe Wong, (4) May Louie, (5) Hank Lai, (6) Dorothy Yee Fong, (7) Peggy Fong Yee, (8) Benny Fong, (9) William Lew, (10) Elizabeth Fong, (11) Betty Dong-Fong, (12) Henry Fong, (13) Robert "Bobby" Fong, (14) Leland Hue, (15) Mardella Yue, (16) Yen Louie, (17) Harry D. Fong, (18) Harry Fong-Yee, (19) Jeannette Jung, and (20) Betty Chan. (Courtesy Roger G. F. and Florence Chan Fong.)

The Wah Yens, a Sacramento Chinese American boys' group had their eighth annual Blossom Time Dance on April 17, 1954. It was held at the Bungalow Inn off Highway 80 (old Roseville Freeway) north of Sacramento. In the picture are, from left to right, Paul Lee, Calvin Jung, Ying Jue, and Barry Lim. (Courtesy Jeanette Leong Fong.)

In 1959, the Wah Yens participated in a bowling tournament in the Los Angeles area. During the tournament, some of the members had time to enjoy themselves in the saloon at Knott's Berry Farm. From left to right are Robin King, Curtis Jang, Ron Lee, Dwayne Lee, Harry Fong, Barry Lim, and Duncan Fong. (Courtesy Robin King.)

Lincoln School filled an extremely significant role in the education of the Chinese American children from the 1920s to the 1960s. The school existed since the late 1800s and was located at Fifth and P Streets. Almost all of the Chinese families in Sacramento lived in or around this area. The school was first named the Franklin Primary School and later changed its name to Lincoln School. Due to a fire, it was rebuilt in 1927 at a cost of half a million dollars. The school was closed in the 1970s. A plaque commemorating the site of the Lincoln School is located at the entry to the California Public Employees' Retirement Systems (CALPERS) building. (Both, courtesy Calvin Jung.)

This is the 1938 kindergarten class at Lincoln School on P Street. Since the neighborhood around the school was predominately Chinese Americans, they represented a large percentage of the class. (Courtesy Jean Fat Lai.)

To ensure safety of the students crossing the streets around Lincoln School, students were used as crossing guards at the pedestrian crosswalks. These are two of the crossing guards from the sixth grade, Ronald Lai, left, and Wesley Lee, right. The picture was taken in 1949. (Courtesy Ronald Lai.)

The Chinese Student Club was a very active organization at Sacramento High School. Above are the members in the 1948–1949 school year. Below are the members of the Chinese Student Club during the 1955–1956 school year at Sacramento High School. From left to right are (first row) Lorraine Fong, Margo Wai, Jane Fong, Helen Fong, Harry Fong, Peggy Lee, Loretta Gin, Sherman Chan, Judy Dong, Helen Seto, Eleanor Fong, Helen Fong, and James Catteral, advisor; (second row) Andrew Lee, Buck Fong, Sylvia Lee, Mary Jang, Jeannette Dong, Alice Fong, Lorraine Fong, Marguerite Fong, Dennis Fong, Sam Fong, and Rolland Fong; (third row) Paul Yee, Barry Lim, Lori Lai, Howard Wong, Herman Lum, Sam Jang, Kenneth Jeong, Gordon Wong, Quock Fong, Henry Wong, and Raymond Yee. (Above, courtesy Betty Chan Fong; below, courtesy Mary Tom.)

Sacramento High School was established in 1856 and was the second-oldest high school in California. The high school moved several times before it finally settled in 1924 at Thirty-fourth and Y Streets, the current location. Most of the Chinese American children in Sacramento attended this high school. This picture was taken in 1924 immediately after the construction of the school. (Courtesy Mary Tom.)

Jai Sei Chi was the Chinese student club at Sacramento City College. The members in 1957 are, from left to right, (first row) Helen Lee, Sandra Fong, Janet Wong, and Alice Fong; (second row) Joan Lai, Helen Wong, Jean Low, Jack Wong, and Richard Chan; (third row) Howard Seto, Tommy Foan, Elwin Jang, and Sherman Chan; (fourth row) Kenneth Tom, Edward Chun, King Fong, and Hobart Fong. (Courtesy Robert W. H. Fong.)

JUNE DANCE
presented by
JAI SEI CHI
sacramento junior college

semi formal	june 15, 1957
nine til one	couples $2.75

hellenic center, 600 alhambra boulevard
wayne shirley and his orchestra

officers, spring 1957

president	richard chan
women's vice president	jo ann lai
men's vice president	tom foon
recording secretary	barbara fong
corresponding secretary	francis wong
treasurer	king fong
publicity	penny lee
representative	marguerite fong
advisors	herb blossom, phillip onstott

june dance committee

co-chairmen	jo ann lai, tom foon
decorations	penny lee
refreshments	richard chan
door	bob mar
contest	jo ann lai
bids	howard seto
hall	richard chan
band	howard seto

miss co-ed of 1957

queen candidates	managers
alice fong	harry sen
barbara fong	marieanne lew
lorraine fong	jim gee
jeannette leong	betty yue
francis wong	harold suen

Jai Sei Chi held their June Dance in 1957 at the Hellenic Center at 600 Alhambra Boulevard. At the dance, Jeanette Leong was crowned that year's Miss Coed. Here she is showing her trophy to Ted Miyagawa. From left to right are Jeanette Leong, Florence Chan, an unidentified student, Shirley Leong, Lyle Lai, Ted Miyagawa, Betty Yue, and Betsy Hom. (Both, courtesy Jeanette Leong Fong.)

China Night, a fund-raiser for charity, was sponsored by the Capitol Lions Club on May 5, 1962. The banquet was held at the Hong King Lum restaurant with the formal event at the Chinese Community Center at Fourth and I Streets. In the performance at the community center below are, from left to right, Joleen ?, DeeDee Jan, Nancy Leong, Barbara Fong, Betty Wong, Doree Fong, and Jeanette Leong (Both, courtesy Jeanette Leong Fong.)

These Kwai Wah classmates formed a team on their own and played teams as far away as Marysville. This picture was taken in 1940. Soon afterwards all the players began their U.S. military service. From left to right are (first row) Fook Fong, Joe Wayne Fong, Leland Chinn, Jack Fong, and Leonard Kwong; (second row) Harry Joe Lee, Arnold Fong, Baron Lowe, David Yee, Raymond Kwong, and Wallace Chan. (Courtesy Harry Joe Lee.)

The Chung Mei Post No. 8358 Veteran of Foreign Wars sponsored this baseball team in Chinatown in 1948. From left to right are (first row) Joe W. Fong, unidentified ballplayer, unidentified ballplayer, and Courtland Chow; (second row) Walter Fong, Russell Fong, Paul Hom, Raymond Kwong, and William Fong. (Courtesy Joe W. Fong.)

In 1951, a group of Chinese American boys in the Sacramento Chinese community formed a baseball team to enter the Sacramento City 110-pound Hardball League. The boys did not have a sponsor or uniforms and used their everyday clothing and shoes to play. Overcoming all odds, at the end of the season, they were the Sacramento City Champions for their league. (Courtesy Jeanette Leong Fong.)

The Chinese American community organized a Boy Scout troop in the 1920s. The scout leader was Harry Y. Wong, back row, second from the right in the scout uniform. This picture was taken in 1926. (Courtesy Janet Wong Chan.)

The Chung Wah Chinese School, after moving to the new facility at 522 M Street, established a drum and bugle corps. This picture was taken in 1935 in front of the school. (Courtesy Roger G. F. Fong.)

The Capitol Lions Club in 1957 sponsored a drum and bugle corps for Boy Scout Troop No. 96. This was an all-Chinese American Boy Scout troop in Sacramento. The instructors were Tommy Fong and Yuk Fong. It later became the Yee Wah and then the current Mandarin Drum and Bugle Corps. (Courtesy Robert W. H. Fong.)

The Sacramento Mandarin Drum and Bugle Corps was founded in 1963. The corps has won many awards, including the prestigious Spirit of Disney Award, signifying outstanding achievement in educational and entertainment program for youth. Here they are performing at the July 4, 1978, parade in Old Sacramento. (Courtesy Eva Chow Fong, Ed.D.)

The Sacramento Mandarin Drum and Bugle Corps was one of the three corps selected from the United States to perform at the inauguration of Chiang Kai-Shek in May 1972. The corps director was Helen Owyang. Madame Chiang Kai-shek, wife of the president of the Republic of China, is in the center of the picture posing with the Sacramento Mandarin and Bugle Corps in Taiwan. (Courtesy Helen Owyang.)

The Sacramento Mandarin Drum and Bugle Corps have taught thousands of young men and women the values of leadership, discipline, and good citizenship. This 1981 picture exemplifies the caliber of the corps. (Courtesy Betty Chan Fong.)

Sacramento's Chinese women were very active in bowling during the 1960s and 1970s. The league, referred to as the Chinese Women's Handicap League, competed at the Alpine Alley on Twenty-fourth Street and Florin Road. This picture was taken around 1967. (Courtesy Betty Chan Fong.)

These two pictures of women in traditional Chinese-style dresses (*cheongsam*) were taken during the grand opening in 1961 of the Confucius Temple at 915 Fourth Street. They were acting as hostesses to greet the many guests during the event. In the picture at left, the hostesses from left to right are (first row) Pat Fong, Penny Lim, and Pauline Joe; (second row) Jeanette Leong and Shirley Leong; (third row) Gladys Louie, Margaret Yee, and Barbara Fong, (fourth row) Betsy Hom, Betty Fong, and unidentified. (Above, courtesy Robert W. H. Fong; left, courtesy Jeanette Leong Fong.)

The 1979 Fat Choy Bazaar (which in later years evolved into the Pacific Rim Street Festival) had a fashion show at the Chinese Cultural Center. From left to right, the following people participated as models: Elaine ?, Vicki Beaton, Eva Fong, the master of ceremony Lester Fong, Tina Byrnes, Elaine ?, Lily Keyser, and unidentified. (Courtesy Eva Chow Fong, Ed.D.)

This Sacramento Chinese golf group was playing in a tournament in Hilo, Hawaii, on September 11, 2001, when the terrorists attacked in New York and Washington, D.C. All airlines flights were cancelled due to security. The Sacramento golfers were stranded on Hilo, Hawaii, all week until security was lifted and the group could schedule a flight back to Sacramento. (Courtesy Dolly Hom.)

Yvonne Fong Soo immigrated to the United States in 1936 with her mother, Fong Yee Wee Ping, and was detained and processed at the Angel Island Immigration Station. She waited 57 years before she could ask her sister, Lana Fong Chong, to return to Angel Island and confront this place. In 1993, twenty family and friends accompanied her on a private tour given by Paul Chow, the activist who fought for the preservation of this historic site to commemorate the immigration of Chinese during the period of the Exclusion Act. The visit on a bright sunny day helped to vanquish those old and frightening memories. Yvonne stands at the center of the wooden portal; Paul stands in the back row, second from the right. Lana Fong Chong is in the first row, wearing a UC Berkeley sweatshirt and a visor. (Courtesy Lana Fong Chong.)

Five

Chinese Americans and China's Opening to the World

America is the world's oldest democracy and the most technologically advanced nation on earth, attracting Chinese here because of these two strengths. In the middle of the 19th century, the Chinese people knew that they needed a change from their repressive imperial government and more changes to address the challenges posed by the West. Many felt that the answer to China's problems would be found in the United States. When gold was discovered in California, China's opening to the world began. Led by miners, merchants, and farmers, the Chinese came to explore the new land. They had already heard about the natural bounty in this new continent and of marvelous inventions like steam locomotives and steamboats. A new form of government with a popularly elected president rather than an emperor who claimed a divine right to rule was also something of great interest to them. Soon, students started coming to America. Yung Wing became the first Chinese man and probably the first Asian, to graduate from an American university when he was granted a bachelor's degree from Yale in 1854. Many more Chinese students would follow, learning math and science from the American university system, the best in the world. These students often stayed in America after their studies, enriching not only the Chinese American community but American society in general. Rebellions against the Manchus became endemic during the middle of the 19th century. All failed against the still powerful Qing. Each time a rebellion failed, many of the rebel leaders were hunted down, tortured, and executed by agents of the emperor. Rather than face certain death in China, many fled to America as political refugees, where they found ready allies in their fight against a common enemy. Sacramento's Chinese Americans supported both the reform movement and the revolution against Manchu domination. A large chapter of the Chinese Empire Reform Association was an important part of Sacramento Chinatown's history. Later when the reform movement failed and the Kuomintang (or Nationalist) party was organized, Sacramento Chinese Americans opened a local office. Part of the rich history of Chinatown is the story of the four Sacramento Chinese Americans who volunteered to serve as bodyguards for Sun Yet-sun after the 1911 revolution.

The Chinese Empire Reform Association (Baohuang hui) was formed in Canada in 1899 by Kang Yu-wei. A chapter was started in Sacramento in 1904. (Courtesy Chinese American Council of Sacramento.)

Chuck Fong (Fong Sik Leong) was born in China and came to America in 1902. He settled in Sacramento and later became a bodyguard for Dr. Sun Yat-sen. This picture was taken in the 1910s. After returning to America, he served as the president in the Sacramento chapter of the Kuomintang. He was also one of the founders of the Sun Yat-sen Memorial Hall and the Confucius Chinese School. (Courtesy Helen Owyang.)

The Kuomintang (Chinese Nationalist Party) was founded in 1912 by Dr. Sun Yat-sen and Sung Chiao-ren. To expand support for the party, chapters were established in America. The Sacramento chapter of the Kuomintang received this certificate in November 1916 and was designated Chapter No. 8. (Courtesy Dr. Herbert Yee and the Sun Yat-sen Memorial Association.)

今查有美國
嘉[illegible]霓彌亞省
沙加緬度埠
國民黨分部
成立於中華民國
庚戌年五月廿一日
照章准予註冊合
給證書永認為本
黨同一團體務期
恪守黨章共圖發
達此証

中國國民黨美洲總支部給

中華民國五年十一月十日

George Fong was born in 1879 in China and came to America in 1897. He returned to China in 1907 and married Ow Shee then came back to America that same year. He joined the Young China Association in 1907. At the meeting, some members volunteered to draw straws to determine who would assassinate Tsai Hsun, a prince of the Manchu government in charge of China's navy, who would be visiting the United States. George drew the short straw, which meant he would have that honor. On October 6, 1910, he was arrested and sentenced to 14 years at San Quentin. After serving 4.5 years, he was paroled in 1915 for good behavior and settled in Sacramento until his death in March 1953. (Both, courtesy Gena Hoyer.)

The Kuomintang was a very active organization in Sacramento during the first half of the 1900s. Many of the local Chinese were members of that organization. This is the membership card in the party for William Yue Fong in 1929. (Courtesy Eva Chow Fong, Ed.D.)

The Fifth National Convention of the Kuomintang chapters in the United States was held in Sacramento on August 28, 1931. Here are the committee members attending the convention. (Courtesy Dr. Herbert Yee and Sun Yat-sen Memorial Association.)

In 1944, the Sacramento chapter of the Kuomintang celebrated the anniversary of the founding of the Kuomintang in China. This picture was taken of the party members and guests in front of their Sacramento office building at 910 Fourth Street. (Courtesy Betty Chan Fong.)

The Sacramento chapter of the Kuomintang was a very active organization. Their meetings generally drew an overflowing crowd of members. This is a picture of one of its meeting in 1949. (Courtesy Robert W. H. Fong.)

蔡廷鍇贈

廷鍇遊歷歐美專為致謝僑胞
援助淞滬抗敵之厚意及考察
各國軍政以增本人學識蒙僑
胞熱烈歡迎且慚且感僑胞既
以抗敵救國歡迎廷鍇廷鍇亦
以抗敵救國相期望今將歸國
爰本古人臨別贈言之義寫此
箴言互相勉勵海天萬里相感
在精神熱血滿腔所期惟切實
抗敵救國箴言

抗要實力責己為宜
敵貨勿用儉德自持
救要真心做人為基
廉恥先立信義歸依
合羣辦事大公無私
勿爭意氣勿亂是非
任怨任勞負責不辭
讓功讓賢成功可期

蔡廷鍇

中華民國二十四年元旦書於金門

Gen. Tsai Ting Kai, commander of the Republic of China's 19th Route Army, was on a goodwill tour through the Central Valley, including Sacramento, in November 1934 to raise funds for China's war victims. He sent this note of appreciation to the overseas Chinese for their support. (Courtesy Ruth Chan Jang.)

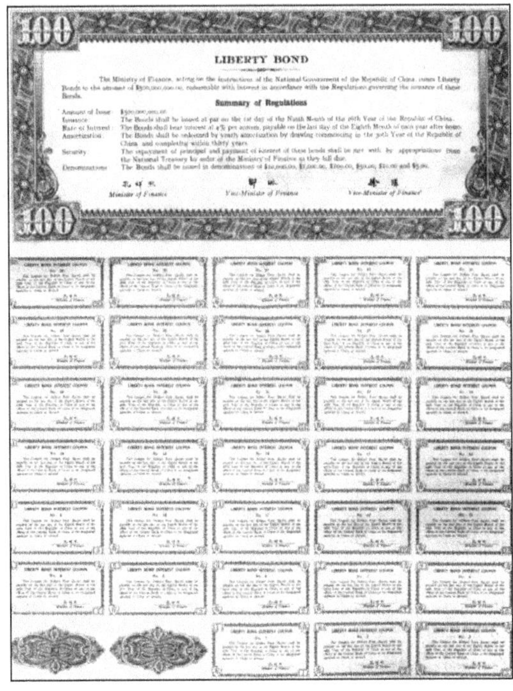

A key source of funding for the Sino-Japanese War was the 1937 sale of liberty bonds issued by the Ministry of Finance of the National Government of the Republic of China. This is a $100 bond with an interest coupon bearing interest at four percent per year. Many of the Chinese Americans in Sacramento purchased these bonds. (Courtesy Lawrence Tom.)

In 1938, Chinese Americans held Rice Bowl campaigns in many cities across the country to raise funds for the victims of the war in China. This was the Rice Bowl float in the Sacramento parade sponsored by the Chinese Women War Service Association in Sacramento. (Courtesy Betty Chan Fong.)

This is the Sacramento Chinese Benevolent Association's planning committee for the annual banquet held for the local Chinese community leaders to celebrate the 40th anniversary of the founding of the Republic of China. The picture was taken on January 7, 1951. (Courtesy Helen Owyang.)

Six

SERVING IN THE MILITARY

For Chinese Americans, World War II started much sooner than for their fellow Americans. Starting in the 1930s, the Chinese American community closely followed the news of Japan's attacks on China, particularly the atrocities committed by Japanese troops in Nanjing. In response, Chinese Americans organized the Chinese War Relief Association to send funds to assist in China's fight against the Japanese. When the United States was attacked by Japan at Pearl Harbor and entered the war, Chinese Americans were ready. Young Chinese American men and women volunteered for the opportunity to fight the Japanese and Germans. Over 22 percent of Chinese American men and women enlisted or were drafted into the armed services, a rate much higher than the 11 percent for the general population. Most were from the first true generation of American-born Chinese, their allegiance firmly established in the land of their birth.

The Chinese American community felt a special obligation to help China in the war. As overseas Chinese living in the most advanced country in the world, they knew that they had skills and abilities that other overseas Chinese did not possess. An important factor in Chinese Americans' support for the war was the fact that the Allies made the war a fight for democracy. Chinese Americans felt that fighting for democracy abroad would help in their fight for equality at home.

One of the most outstanding stories about the bravery of Sacramento's Chinese American men and women in combat involves the three Lee brothers. All three brothers fought in the Korean War, served as officers, and were awarded medals for bravery. Kurt Chew-Een Lee, the oldest, joined as a marine. He was awarded the Navy Cross, the second-highest military medal in the U.S. armed services. Chew-Mon Lee was awarded the Distinguished Service Cross (the army equivalent of the Navy Cross) while serving as a lieutenant in the army. This medal is also the second-highest military award. Chew-Fan Lee served as a lieutenant in the Army Medical Service and received a Bronze Star for bravery. Their heroism in combat was recognized by the California Military Museum when it opened an exhibit on their military exploits in the year 2000.

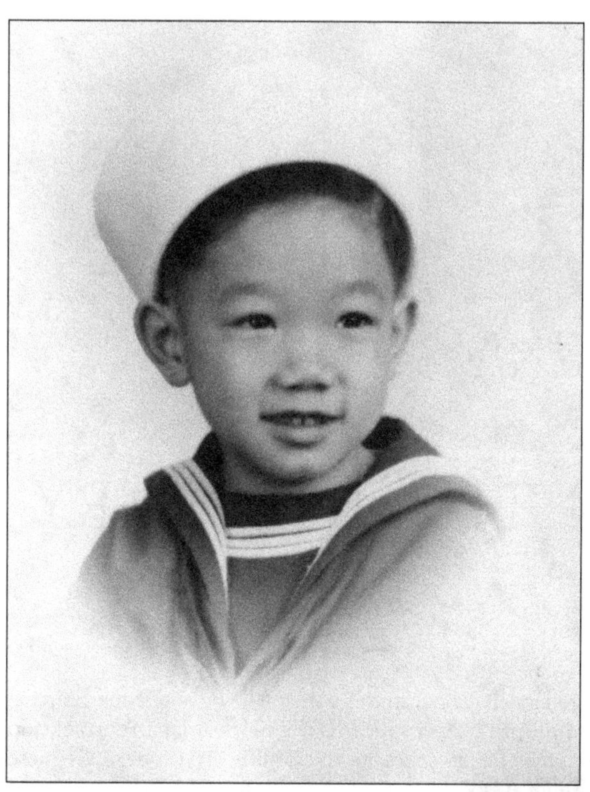

Many Chinese American children were dressed in military uniforms during World War II. This is a picture of Gordon Wong, son of Harry Y. Wong and Yee Shai Wun, dressed in a navy uniform. (Courtesy Merrily Fong Wong.)

Quan Y. Luke was born in China and settled in Sacramento in 1941. He was in an Army Elite Tank Destroyer Unit stationed at Fort Hood during World War II. After the war, he worked at the Sacramento Army Depot. In 1958, he was sent to Laos by the army to advise members of the Laotian Army in the repair and maintenance of radio/radar equipment. (Courtesy Roger G. F. and Florence Fong.)

The Chung Mei Post No. 8358, Veteran of Foreign Wars, was established in October 1946 in Sacramento. The inaugural meeting for this post was at the Clunie Clubhouse at McKinley Park. The first commander of the post was Albert W. Dong. The vice commanders were Benjamin M. B. Louie and Joe Larry Fong Jr. Pictured here is the swearing-in ceremony for the members. (Courtesy Joe W. Fong.)

The Chung Mei Post No. 8358 participated in the November 1946 Veterans Day Parade. Their participation is shown here on J Street between Ninth and Tenth Streets. (Courtesy Joe W. Fong.)

Howard Louie (Gin H. Yim) immigrated to the United States in 1941. He was inducted into the army in 1942 and was a machine gunner in the 84th Division, 335th Battalion. He was captured by the Germans and was a POW at Stalag 2A. After he was discharged from the army, he was awarded the Bronze Star Medal for meritorious service. (Courtesy Easter Jang.)

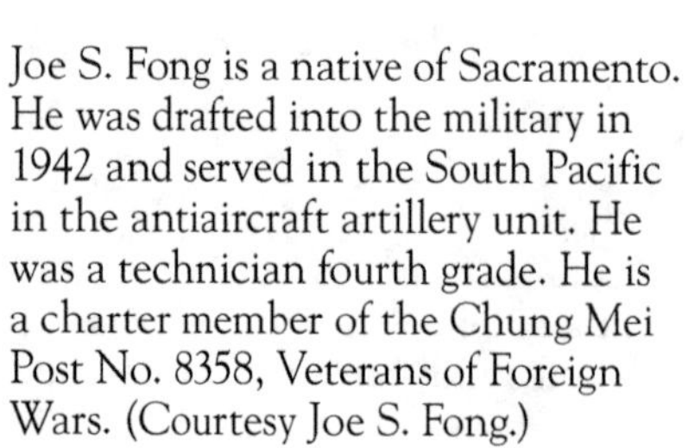

Joe S. Fong is a native of Sacramento. He was drafted into the military in 1942 and served in the South Pacific in the antiaircraft artillery unit. He was a technician fourth grade. He is a charter member of the Chung Mei Post No. 8358, Veterans of Foreign Wars. (Courtesy Joe S. Fong.)

Joe Wayne Fong is a native of Sacramento. He entered the service in 1944 in the armor unit. He was in Germany during World War II as the 50-caliber machine gunner in the Lead Vehicle 773rd Tank Destroyer Battalion Recon Company. He is a charter member of the Chung Mei Post No. 8358, Veterans of Foreign Wars. (Courtesy Joe W. Fong.)

Yen W. Fong was born in China. He immigrated to American in 1926 and settled with his parents in Sacramento. He was in the navy during World War II in the Pacific Ocean on an LST (tank landing ship). After his discharge from the navy, he worked at Sheu Fong Poultry for his father and later opened Archway Market in Rio Linda. (Courtesy Robert W. H. Fong.)

Gung Ho Post 696 American Legion was established in Sacramento in 1946. The post was comprised of all Chinese American veterans. This is the swearing-in ceremony for the members at the first meeting in the Fort Sutter Post Building at Twenty-first and L Streets. Tim Jang was the post's first commander. (Courtesy Frank L. Wong.)

Frank Lee Wong is a native of Sacramento. He entered the army in June 1943. He served as a T-4 grade medical lab technician. After his discharge from the service in May 1946, he worked at McClellan Air Force Base. In 1956, he started working in the Sacramento County Assessor Office and remained there until his retirement in 1984 as a senior property appraiser. (Courtesy Frank L. Wong.)

Ruth Chan was born in Locke and came to Sacramento to attend City College in 1941. She joined the U.S. Air Force in 1943 and was initially assigned to Moody Air Force Base (AFB) in Georgia where there were no other Chinese around. She later transferred to Mitchell AFB in New York and after being discharged, she married Harry Jang in 1947. They settled in Sacramento in 1950. (Courtesy Ruth Chan Jang.)

John Sing Jr. was the second son of John Sing and Cheong Yee Sing. He was born in Sacramento and went into the service during World War II. He was stationed at Camp Beale in 1943 and achieved the rank of technical sergeant. (Courtesy Art B. and Barbara Tom.)

During the Korean War, the September 1950 battle for Inchon was a decisive Allied victory and a strategic reversal in the war. After the Allies had successfully secured the city, by chance, two brothers, Chew Mon-Lee and "Kurt" Chew En-Lee, reunited on the battlefield for a few hours. This meeting was reported in the *Sacramento Bee*. (Courtesy Betty Lee Mar.)

"Kurt" Chew-Een Lee was born in Sacramento. He enlisted in the U.S. Marine Corps in 1944. For his extraordinary heroism during the Korean War, he received the navy's second-highest combat award, the Navy Cross. He retired as a major in the marines. In the picture he represents the Legion of Valor while meeting with Pres. George W. Bush in 2007. (Courtesy Betty Lee Mar.)

Chew-Mon Lee was born in Sacramento. During the Korean War, he is shown receiving the army's second-highest award, the Distinguished Service Cross from Brig. Gen. Carter Clarke. He was the first Chinese American to serve as a military attaché in the State Department. He died on active duty while stationed on Taiwan. He achieved the rank of colonel in the U.S. Army. (Courtesy Betty Lee Mar.)

Chew-Fan Lee was born in Sacramento. He graduated from the University of California College of Pharmacy in 1951 and entered the military service later that year. He was a first lieutenant with the 45th Infantry Division, Army Medical Service in Korea and was awarded the Bronze Star for heroism in Korea after the Inchon campaign. (Courtesy Betty Lee Mar.)

Roger G. F. Fong is a native of Sacramento. After graduating from CSUS in 1956, he joined the navy and was on active duty as a machinist mate 2nd class (MM2) from 1956 to 1958, serving on the first of the new Forrestal class of super carriers in the Mediterranean. The USS *Forrestal* CVA-59 was the biggest warship in the world at that time. (Courtesy Roger G. F. Fong.)

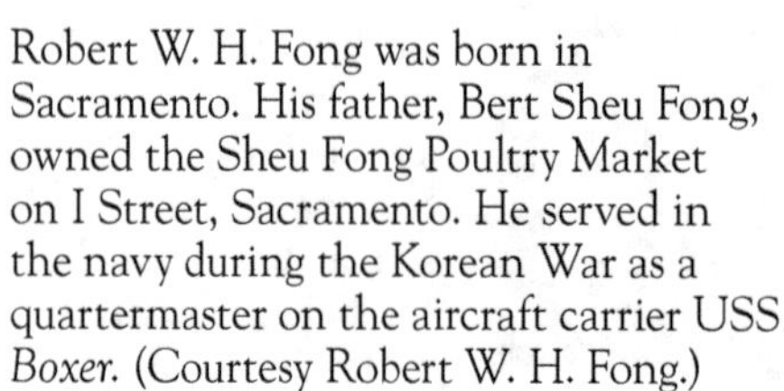

Robert W. H. Fong was born in Sacramento. His father, Bert Sheu Fong, owned the Sheu Fong Poultry Market on I Street, Sacramento. He served in the navy during the Korean War as a quartermaster on the aircraft carrier USS *Boxer.* (Courtesy Robert W. H. Fong.)

William Henry Chan was born in Sacramento's Chinatown at 222 I Street. He attended the University of California at Berkeley and completed his medical training at the University of California at San Francisco medical school for his doctor of medicine. He was a captain in the air force, stationed in Japan, from 1963 to 1966. After his discharge from the military, he returned to Sacramento. He is married to Janet Wong. (Courtesy Dr. William Henry Chan.)

Bill Jang, born and raised in Sacramento, served in Vietnam from 1967 to 1968 with the elite fighting group of Airborne Rangers of the 173rd Airborne Brigade. He was also one of the few who graduated from the highly respected MACV Recondo School conducted by the 5th Special Forces Group. Bill is a life member of the Veterans of Foreign War, Disabled Veterans, and the 75th Ranger Regiment Association. (Courtesy Bill Jang.)

John Chow was born in Sacramento. He was a 1966 graduate from U.S. Naval Officer Candidate School and the U.S. Civil Engineers Officers School. He served in Okinawa and later Vietnam. In Vietnam, Lt. John Chow was company commander of Naval Construction Battalion Maintenance Unit. (Courtesy Eva Chow Fong, Ed.D.)

Gordon A. Wong received his medical degree from UCLA and was drafted into the U.S. Army. He served in Germany with the 24th Infantry, First Battalion, 70th Armor, where he achieved the rank of major before his discharge. He is a board certified physician in internal medicine, infectious diseases, and pulmonary medicine in private practice and a clinical professor of medicine at University of California, Davis. (Courtesy Merrily Fong Wong.)

Seven

Becoming American

World War II had a major impact on the Chinese American community's struggle to enter mainstream America. Once an isolated and ignored community, the labor shortage and the need for men and women in the armed services forced America to unite all her people. When Chinese American men and women completed their military service at the end of the war, they could no longer accept second-class citizenship in civilian life. Returning servicemen came home looking for opportunities in employment and education. Many furthered their education on the GI Bill by enrolling in colleges or professional schools. Others sought work, often as civil servants because they knew that in the civil service system, they would be treated fairly by their employers. Civil service positions were readily available in state government because of Sacramento's status as the state capital. The nearby McClellan Air Force Base provided more possibilities in federal employment.

Medicine has always played an important role in the Chinese American community. The original Chinatown had many herbalist shops where herbalist and Chinese doctors could diagnose, prescribe, and sell medicine to their patients. In 1934, Dr. Lung Fung became the first Chinese American doctor to practice Western medicine in Sacramento. He was joined a decade later when Dr. George Lee opened his practice. Today Chinese American physicians serve in many medical positions, from the president of the local medical society, to professorships and chairs at the UC Davis Medical School.

In the 1960s, a breakthrough in political participation took place when Sun G. Wong became the first Chinese American to be elected to the Sacramento City Council. Thomas Chinn, elected first as a school board member in 1972 and then subsequently to the city council, followed him. Roger Fong was elected to serve as Sacramento County assessor in 1986, the first Chinese American assessor in the United States. Jimmy Yee was elected to the city council in 1992, served for a time as mayor, and was later elected to Sacramento County Board of Supervisors. A minority once denied the vote because they could not become naturalized citizens, Chinese Americans are now an important part of Sacramento's political process.

Sun G. Wong was born in China and came to America in 1939 at the age of six. He graduated from California State University at Sacramento in 1955 with a bachelor of arts degree. He was in the real estate business and was the first minority to be elected to Sacramento City Council. He served from 1967 to 1972. (Courtesy Sun G. Wong.)

Thomas Chinn was elected to the Sacramento School Board in 1972. He was then elected to the Sacramento City Council in 1983 to represent District 4, the western central area of the city. He served from 1984 through 1992. He is shown here with Mayor Anne Rudin. (Courtesy Thomas Chinn.)

George Chan was born and raised in Sacramento. In 1969, George was nominated for Best Art Direction at the 42nd Annual Motion Picture Academy Awards in the comedy musical *Gaily Gaily*. He was the art director in over two dozen movies and many television programs, including such series as *The Streets of San Francisco*, the *The Virginian*, and *Highway to Heaven*. He is married to Bertha Waugh. (Courtesy Bertha Waugh Chan.)

When Merrily Fong Wong became president of the Junior League of Sacramento (1982), a representative of the national organization told her that she was the first woman of color to be in that position in the United States. She was also the first person of Asian descent to be president of the Sacramento Region Community Foundation (1992) and chair of the Mercy Foundation Board of Trustees (2009). (Courtesy Merrily Fong Wong.)

Roger G. F. Fong started his career in the Sacramento County Assessor's Office in 1960. He was elected Sacramento County assessor in 1986, the first minority elected to a county-wide office and the first Chinese assessor in the United States. He was reelected in 1991. He is shown here with his wife, Florence, in 1991. (Courtesy Roger G. F. Fong.)

Jimmie Yee is a native of Sacramento. He was elected in 1992 to the Sacramento City Council and was reelected in 1996 and 2000. In 1999, he was unanimously selected by the city council to serve as the mayor of Sacramento. In 2006, he was the first Chinese American elected to the Sacramento County Board of Supervisors. From left to right are Mary Yee, Jimmie Yee, Jeanette Chan, and Dave Moy. (Courtesy Jimmie Yee.)

The 1962 graduating class at UCSF School of Dentistry included the two Wong sisters, Janet and Julie. They were two of the first female dentists in the Sacramento area. Janet practiced pediatric dentistry, and Julie became an orthodontist. During their education at the School of Dentistry, they were the only women in their classes. William Henry Chan, Janet's husband, also graduated from UCSF medical school in 1962. (Courtesy Janet Wong Chan.)

Cynthia (Cindy) Hom Goodman was born and raised in Sacramento. She was valedictorian of Sacramento High School's class of 1985. She was the first Chinese American female to become chief resident of plastic surgery at Baylor College of Medicine in Houston, Texas. She was also the first Chinese American to become chief of plastic surgery at Marin General Hospital in Marin County, California. (Courtesy Leonard Hom, Ph.D.)

Edna (Gin) Louie was born and raised in Sacramento. She was crowned homecoming queen at Sacramento High School in 1967. In the 111 years since the establishment of Sacramento High School, she was only the second minority to achieve the honor of being named homecoming queen. (Courtesy Easter Jang.)

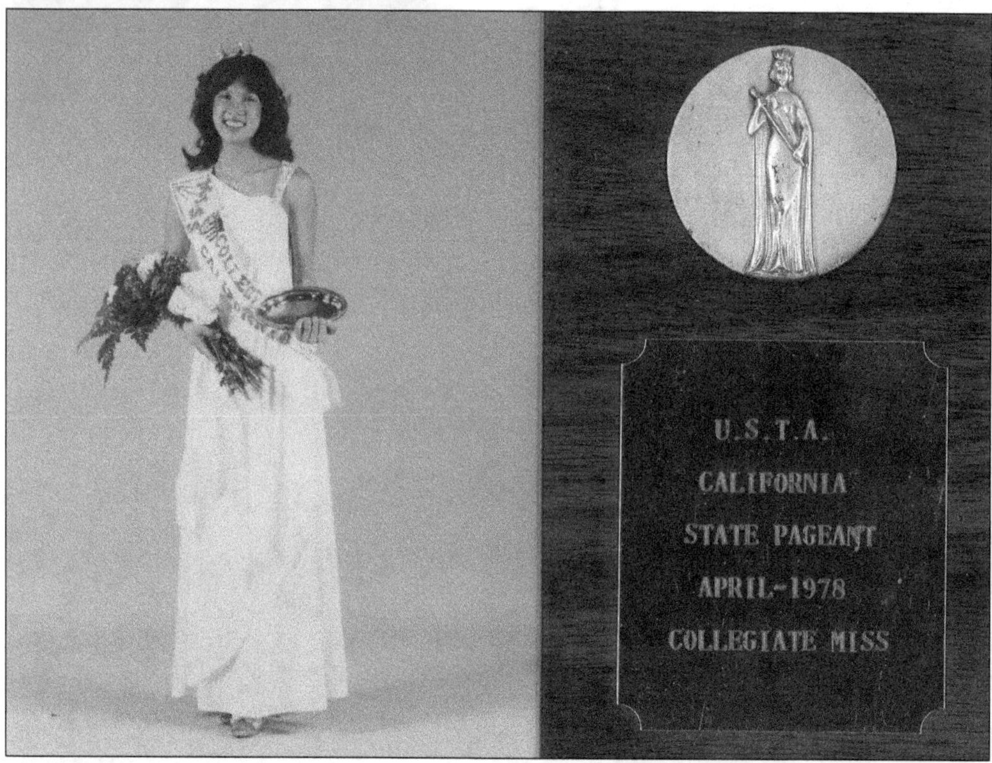

Elizabeth Owyang was born and raised in Sacramento. She was a baton-twirling champion with over 500 trophies and the first Chinese American U.S. Twirling Association judge in the mid-1980s. She is a physician and chief of the Ophthalmology Department at Kaiser in Bellflower. (Courtesy Helen Owyang.)

Rob King Fong is a third-generation Chinese American in Sacramento. After completing his education, he began his career as an attorney and later was a partner at Ryan and Fong. He was elected to the Sacramento City Unified School Board in 1998. In 2004, he was elected to the Sacramento City Council and in 2006 was selected as vice mayor. Fong was reelected in June 2008. (Courtesy Rob King Fong.)

Eric Mar, the son of Richard and Betty Mar, was born and raised in Sacramento. He is an attorney and an associate professor at San Francisco State University. In 2000, he was elected to the San Francisco Board of Education and later became the board president. In November 2008, he was elected to the San Francisco County Board of Supervisors. (Courtesy Betty Lee Mar.)

Deborah Tom was born and raised in Sacramento. She received her pediatric training from Baylor College of Medicine in Houston and a Neonatology Fellowship at Stanford University. She is a member of the Board of Directors for Neonatology Associates, LTD, the largest neonatology group in Arizona. Here she is giving Sen. John McCain a tour of the Phoenix Children's Hospital's Neonatal ICU in July 2009. (Courtesy Deborah J. Tom, M.D.)

Lawrence Tom is a third-generation Chinese American. He graduated from CSUS in 1959 and started his career in California state government in 1961. In 1994, he was appointed California's first and only accounting administrator IV (principal level), the highest-level accounting classification possible. He was subsequently elevated to a career executive assignment (CEA). He managed a staff of over 600.

Eight

Preserving the Past, Anticipating the Future

Throughout Chinese American history, the Chinese have learned much from America. All great civilizations need to be open to new ideas if they are to remain great. The Chinese forgot this important lesson in the latter part of the Qing Dynasty. It took them more than a century to correct this mistake. Now as China undergoes its renaissance as a great civilization, perhaps America will be learning much from China. Chinese American pioneers introduced the Western world to the richness of the Chinese civilization. They brought two major religions, Buddhism and Taoism, to the North America continent and built a series of temples throughout the American West. They showed Americans new ways to prepare food using natural and fresh ingredients. Their medical practices cured conditions for which Western medicine had no remedies. They retaught the lessons of loyalty to family and friends so necessary during the period of discriminatory immigration laws that separated Chinese Americans from their loved ones. Even today, their respect for learning is an inspiration for many Americans. The Sacramento Chinese American community has changed over the years, but it still retains its vitality and sense of purpose. Eleven Chinese American associations are active in Sacramento today, each dedicated to serving the needs of its members. Among them, the Sacramento Sun Yat-sen Memorial Association has made its goal the teaching of Chinese history and culture and the passing on of this knowledge to the next generation. The Friends of the Yee Fow Museum was organized in 2007 to build a museum that would preserve Chinese American history and serve as a link to a new China. In June 2007, they organized a presentation before the California Senate Select Committee on Asian Pacific Islander Affairs, chaired by Sen. Leland Yee, to make state officials aware of the necessity for creating a Chinese American museum. Committee leaders and historians spoke at this hearing, urging support for this new museum. In the fall of 2009, the annual Chinatown Mall Culture Fair picked as its theme, "Bridging the Past to the Future." As it has throughout its history, Sacramento's Chinese American community continues as a leader in bringing understanding between the Chinese and American peoples.

The Chinese Benevolent Association is located at 915 Fourth Street in the Chinese Confucius Church Building. The association was founded in 1934, and its 11 member groups are the Soo Yuen Ben Association, Yee Fung Toy Association, Wong's Family Benevolent Association, Ong Ko Met Association, Lee On Dong Association, Gee Guck Sam Tuck Association, Gee How Oak Ten Association, Lim Association, Bing Kong Tong, Sun Yat-Sen Memorial Association, and Kuomintang. Below are the members of the board of directors of the Sacramento Chinese Benevolent Association in 2008. The chairman of the board, Dr. Jong L. Chen, is in the first row, fifth from the left. (Both, courtesy Hon Lam.)

The Sacramento Chinese Benevolent Association and the Overseas Chinese Associations welcome a delegation from Hawaii to Sacramento. This picture was taken on July 5, 1955. The reception was held upstairs in the banquet room at the Hong King Lum restaurant on I Street. (Courtesy Jean Fat Lai.)

Bing Kong Tong is located at 918 Fifth Street. The building was part of the redevelopment of Chinatown Mall. The organization was established in the late 1800s in Sacramento. Dr. Sun Yat-sen was reported to have written a portion of the Chinese constitution in an upstairs room of the prior building of Bing Kong Tong on I Street.

Above is a picture of the officials of the Bing Kong Tong Association during the grand opening celebration of their building at 910–914 Third Street (west side) in 1949. The picture below shows the members of Bing Kong Tong Association at the grand opening in front of the building. (Both, courtesy Dr. William Henry Chan.)

Gee How Oak Tin Association is located at 2736 X Street. It was established in Sacramento in 2001. The membership is open to descendants of the Chan, Woo, and Yuen families. (Courtesy Hon Lam.)

Gee Tak Sam Tak Association is located at 926 T Street. This organization was established in 1920 on Third Street and later moved to its present location. It includes families with the surname of Wu, Cheu, Choy, Yang, and Tsao.

This is the ground breaking in 1960 for the current Lim Family Association building located at 2101 Ninth Street, the southeast corner of Ninth and U Streets. The participants from left to right are, unidentified, Jack Chew, and Yue Lim (Lim Gon Yue). The completed building is shown below. (Both, courtesy Virginia Lim Hashisaka.)

The Lee Family Association was established in 1870s Sacramento. The name was later changed in 1947 to the Lee On Dong Association. Initially, it was located in a rented facility at 401½ I Street. After moving several times, the association in 1946 constructed a building at 304 J Street, which was demolished in 1965 for redevelopment. The association is presently located at 2014 Ninth Street in a building purchased in 1982.

Ong Ko Met Association moved to its present location at 427 J Street in 1972. It was established in 1942 at 973 Third Street.

The Wong Family Benevolent Association, located at 1702 Broadway, was initially established in Sacramento in 1875.

The Sun Yat-sen Memorial Association is located at 415 Chinatown Mall. The Memorial Center was built in 1971 in the Chinatown Mall. The goals of the Sun Yat-sen Center are to preserve Chinese heritage and to study Dr. Sun's philosophy, beliefs, and principles. (Courtesy Mary Tom.)

The Sun Yat-sen Memorial Hall located at 415 Chinatown Mall was dedicated on June 6, 1971. The master of ceremonies was Li Yen Chan and the ribbon cutting was done by William Yue Fong, president of the Sun Yat-sen Association. There were many public officials present, including U.S. Sen. Hiram L. Fong of Hawaii. The introductions were in both English and Chinese, provided by Dr. Herbert Yee and Howard L. Wong, respectively. (Both, courtesy Dr. Herbert Yee and the Sun Yat-sen Association.)

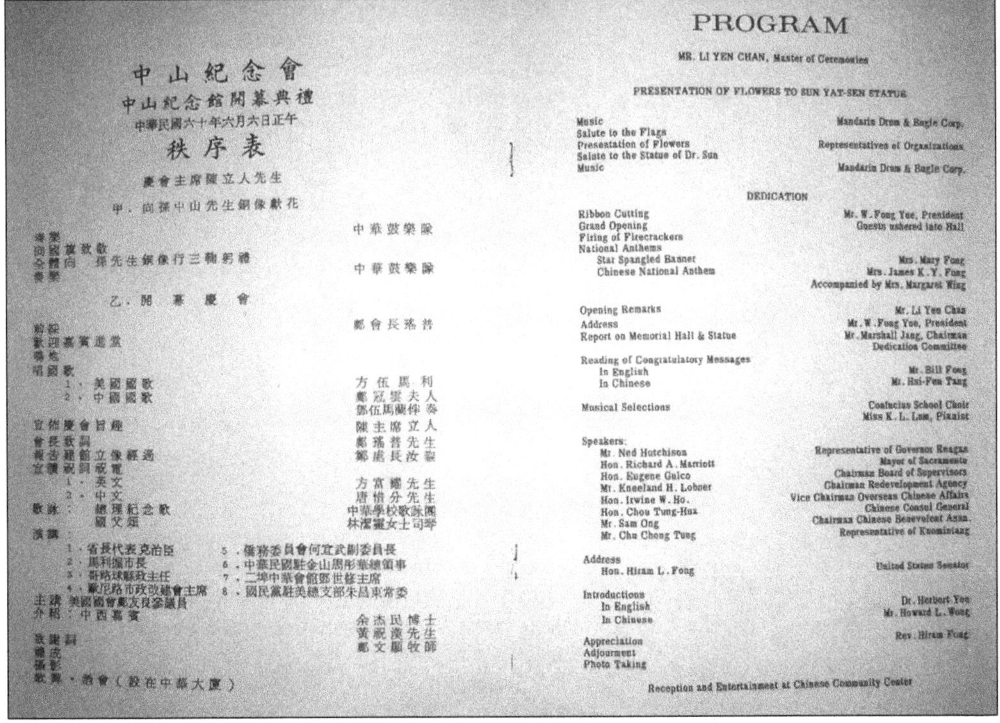

中山紀念會
中山紀念館開幕典禮
中華民國六十年六月六日正午
秩序表
慶會主席陳立人先生

甲、向孫中山先生銅像獻花

奏樂 — 中華鼓樂隊
向國旗致敬
全體向孫先生銅像行三鞠躬禮
奏樂 — 中華鼓樂隊

乙、開幕慶會

剪綵 — 鄺會長瑞普
歡迎嘉賓進堂
鳴炮
唱國歌
1、美國國歌 — 方伍馬利
2、中國國歌 — 鄺冠堅夫人
鄧伍馬蘭伴奏
宣佈慶會旨趣 — 陳主席立人
會長致詞 — 鄺瑞普先生
報告建館立像經過 — 鄭處長汝鎏
宣讀祝詞祝電
1、英文 — 方富耀先生
2、中文 — 唐惜分先生
歌詠：總理紀念歌
國父頌 — 中華學校歌詠團
林潔靈女士司琴
演講：
1、省長代表克治臣
2、馬利握市長
3、哥略球縣政主任
4、歐尼路市政改建會主席
5、僑務委員會何宜武副委員長
6、中華民國駐金山周彤華總領事
7、二埠中華會館鄧世修主席
8、國民黨駐美總支部朱昌東常委
主講 美國國會鄺友良參議員
介紹：中西嘉賓 — 余杰民博士
黃祝漢先生
致謝詞 — 鄺文顯牧師
禮成
攝影
歡宴・酒會（設在中華大廈）

PROGRAM

MR. LI YEN CHAN, Master of Ceremonies

PRESENTATION OF FLOWERS TO SUN YAT-SEN STATUE

Music — Mandarin Drum & Bugle Corp.
Salute to the Flags
Presentation of Flowers — Representatives of Organizations
Salute to the Statue of Dr. Sun
Music — Mandarin Drum & Bugle Corp.

DEDICATION

Ribbon Cutting — Mr. W. Fong Yee, President
Grand Opening — Guests ushered into Hall
Firing of Firecrackers
National Anthems
Star Spangled Banner — Mrs. Mary Fong
Chinese National Anthem — Mrs. James K.Y. Fong
Accompanied by Mrs. Margaret Wing

Opening Remarks — Mr. Li Yen Chan
Address — Mr. W. Fong Yee, President
Report on Memorial Hall & Statue — Mr. Marshall Jang, Chairman Dedication Committee

Reading of Congratulatory Messages
In English — Mr. Bill Fong
In Chinese — Mr. Hsi-Fen Tang

Musical Selections — Confucius School Choir
Miss K. L. Lam, Pianist

Speakers:
Mr. Ned Hutchison — Representative of Governor Reagan
Hon. Richard A. Marriott — Mayor of Sacramento
Hon. Eugene Gulco — Chairman Board of Supervisors
Mr. Kneeland H. Lobner — Chairman Redevelopment Agency
Hon. Irwine W. Ho. — Vice Chairman Overseas Chinese Affairs
Hon. Chou Tung-Hua — Chinese Consul General
Mr. Sam Ong — Chairman Chinese Benevolent Assn.
Mr. Chu Chong Tung — Representative of Kuomintang

Address
Hon. Hiram L. Fong — United States Senator

Introductions
In English — Dr. Herbert Yee
In Chinese — Mr. Howard L. Wong

Appreciation — Rev. Hiram Fong
Adjournment
Photo Taking

Reception and Entertainment at Chinese Community Center

The Soo Yuen Association is located at 401 J Street. The association consists of three families, Louie, Fong, and Kwong. The association's headquarters was founded in San Francisco in 1880. The Sacramento branch was established in 1919.

In the mid-1930s, William Yue Fong played the part of German emperor Wilhelm Kaiser in the Chinese New Year parade celebration at the Soo Yuen Benevolent Association since there was no one else who wanted that role. Subsequent to this role, he became known as Kaiser Bill in the Chinese community. (Courtesy Eva Chow Fong, Ed.D.)

PROGRAM

OFFICIAL OPENING CEREMONY IN COMMEMORATION OF THE NEW EDIFICE

SOO YUEN BENEVOLENT ASSOCIATION

401 JAY STREET, SACRAMENTO, CALIFORNIA 95814

May 17, 1970 - Commencing 12:00 Noon

Co-masters of Ceremonies

JIM Y. LOUIE, Chinese Linguist; WILLIAM J. FONG, English Linguist.

11:30 sharp: Assembly of the Chinese Community
Drum & Bugle Corps
Front Entrance of the Association in Parade.

1. Fire Crackers and Music by Chinese Band, San Francisco.
2. The Lion Dance – Directed by RAYMOND KWONG.
3. Anthems: MRS. JAMES K. FONG.
4. Unveiling of Curtain in Altar.
5. Salute to the Flag.
6. Past and the Future: The Co-masters of Ceremonies.
7. Welcome Speech:
   JIMMY FONG, President of the Association.
   LOUIE FAT TAO, Grand President.
8. Brief Remarks:
   WALTER FONG, Chairman of Building Committee.
9. Congratulatory Messages from Chinese Officials:
   HON. W. FONG YUE, Member of National Board of Control
   HON. CHOW TUNG-HUA, Consul General of the Republic of China, San Francisco
   Grand President of the Chinese Six Companies, San Francisco
   SAM ONG, President of Chinese Benevolent Association of Sacramento
10. Chinese Selection for the Dedication –
11. Official Recognition from:
   HON. RONALD REAGAN, Governor of State of California
   HON. JOHN E. MOSS, Congressman, Third District
   HON. HENRY KLOSS, Chairman, Board of Supervisors
   HON. MICHAEL S. SANDS, Vice City Mayor of Sacramento
   HON. KNEELAND H. LOBNER, Redevelopment Agency
12. Reading of Congratulatory Messages and Telegrams:
   JON LEWIS FONG in Chinese;
   BENJAMIN LOUIE in English.
13. The Introduction of Honor Guests:
   American Guests by REV. HIRAM FONG;
   Chinese Guests by WING LOUIS.
14. Appreciation:
   In Chinese by JAMES K. FONG;
   In English by BENJAMIN LOUIE.
15. Adjournment – Followed by: Tea Party and Taking of Pictures.

Banquet and Entertainment Program
At Chinese Community Center – 5:00 P.M.

The Soo Yuen Benevolent Association had the grand opening of their new building at 401 J Street on May 17, 1970. Attendees to the event included California governor Ronald Reagan and John E. Moss, congressman from the Third District. (Both, courtesy Helen Owyang.)

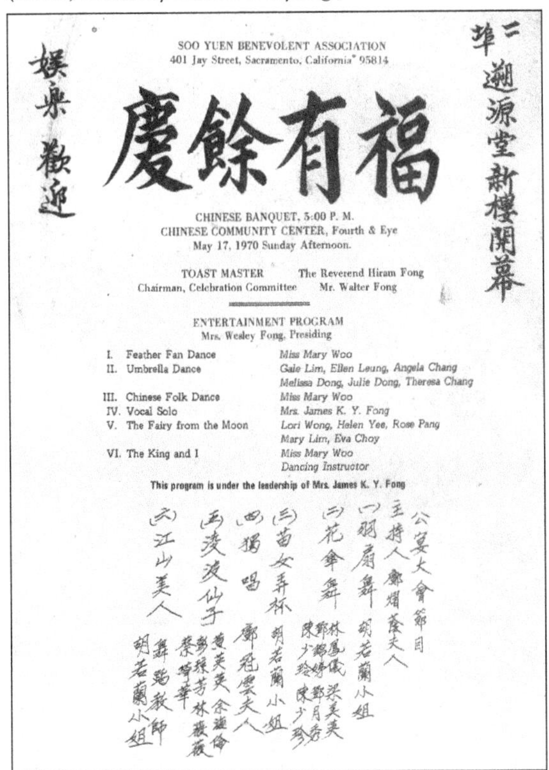

二埠遡源堂新樓開幕

SOO YUEN BENEVOLENT ASSOCIATION
401 Jay Street, Sacramento, California 95814

娛樂歡迎

福有餘慶

CHINESE BANQUET, 5:00 P. M.
CHINESE COMMUNITY CENTER, Fourth & Eye
May 17, 1970 Sunday Afternoon.

TOAST MASTER The Reverend Hiram Fong
Chairman, Celebration Committee Mr. Walter Fong

ENTERTAINMENT PROGRAM
Mrs. Wesley Fong, Presiding

I.	Feather Fan Dance	*Miss Mary Woo*
II.	Umbrella Dance	*Gale Lim, Ellen Leung, Angela Chang, Melissa Dong, Julie Dong, Theresa Chang*
III.	Chinese Folk Dance	*Miss Mary Woo*
IV.	Vocal Solo	*Mrs. James K. Y. Fong*
V.	The Fairy from the Moon	*Lori Wong, Helen Yee, Rose Pang, Mary Lim, Eva Choy*
VI.	The King and I	*Miss Mary Woo, Dancing Instructor*

This program is under the leadership of Mrs. James K. Y. Fong

公宴大會節目
主持人 鄺熠蓁夫人
(一) 羽扇舞 胡若蘭小姐
(二) 花傘舞 林鳳儀 梁美美 鄭錦婷 鄭月秀 陳少玲 陳少珍
(三) 苗女弄杯 胡若蘭小姐
(四) 獨唱 鄺冠雲夫人
(五) 凌波仙子 黃芙芙 余旋倫 彭綠芳 林薇薇 蔡瑋華
(六) 江山美人 舞蹈教師 胡若蘭小姐

Yee Fung Toy Family Association is located at 1233 Broadway. It is a branch of the Yee Fung Toy Family Association, which began in San Francisco over 100 years ago. The Sacramento branch was established in the latter part of the 1940s.

The Senate Select Committee on Asian Pacific Islander Affairs, chaired by state senator Leland Yee, Ph.D. (D-San Francisco/San Mateo), had a hearing in June 2007 on the proposed Yee Fow Museum. Presentations were made by Steve Yee, Jimmie Yee, Phil Choy, and Brian Tom. The rail yard, which is in the same area as Sacramento's first Chinatown, is a 240-acre site set for redevelopment. (Courtesy Wei Liu, *World Journal*.)

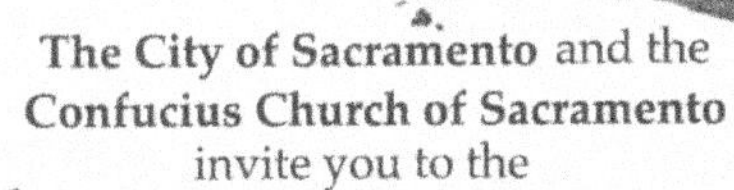

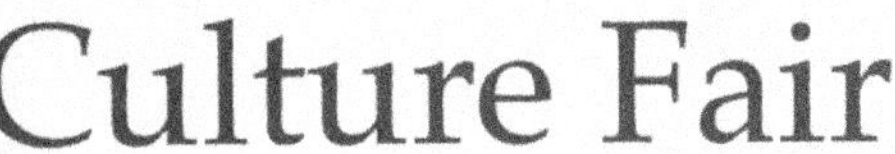

Bridging the Past to the Future

Sacramento Chinatown Mall
3rd - 5th and I - J Streets

Sunday, September 27, 2009
11am - 4 pm

Stage Programs

- Lion Dance
- Chinese Martial Arts
- Chinese Music and Dances
- Chinese Fashion Show

Special Programs

- Noted Author's Stories from Chinatown
- Experience Angel Island Immigrant Statio
- Enjoy Delicious Harvest Mooncakes
- Visit the Sun Yet Sen Memorial Museum

Community Services

- Energy Conservation Resources
- Explore Chinese Medicine / Healing Arts

Demonstrations and Hands On Activities

- Calligraphy
- Origami
- Chinese Lanterns
- Mahjong
- Chinese Chess
- Tai Chi
- Chinese Cooking

Exhibit Booths

- Chinese Music, Videos, and Books
- Chinese Food, Herbs, and Snacks
- Games and Toys
- Cosmetics and Accessories
- Chinese Arts and Crafts
- Corporate Information
- Organizational Information

Children Games,
Guest Speakers,
and Much More

The third annual Chinatown Mall Culture Fair was held on September 27, 2009. The theme was "Bridging the Past to the Future," an expression of the Chinese culture and a recognition of the journey and contribution of Chinese immigrants to America. It was a huge success and drew a large crowd from all over northern California. Everyone enjoyed a day of Chinese culture, arts and Chinese-Californian history. There was also a special exhibit featuring the Angel Island Immigration Station where an estimated 175,000 Chinese were processed. The exhibit, Gateway to Gold Mountain (Gim Shan), is a tribute to the pioneering spirit of all those who persevered and established new roots in America. (Courtesy Steve Yee.)

www.ingramcontent.com/pod-product-compliance
Lightning Source LLC
LaVergne TN
LVHW081554100826
845153LV00004B/381

* 9 7 8 1 5 3 1 6 5 3 3 7 8 *